#14291902

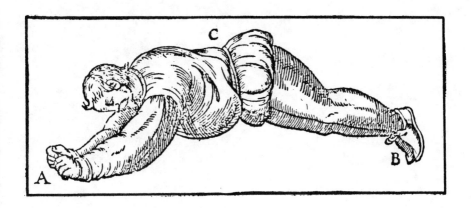

THE DANCING BODY IN RENAISSANCE CHOREOGRAPHY
(c. 1416-1589)

THE DANCING BODY IN RENAISSANCE CHOREOGRAPHY
(c. 1416-1589)

by
Mark Franko

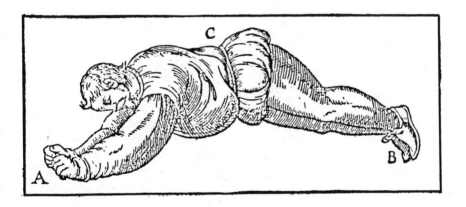

SUMMA PUBLICATIONS, INC.
Birmingham, Alabama
1986

Printed in the United States of America
Library of Congress Catalog Card Number 85-61602
ISBN 0-917786-39-4

To my parents

TABLE OF CONTENTS

I would like to express my gratitude to Michael Riffaterre for his critical vigilance, encouragement and support. I would also like to thank Columbia University, the Ecole Normale Supérieure of the rue d'Ulm (Paris) and the Whiting Foundation without whose aid this project could not have reached completion.

M.F.

"Je vous ai dit plus haut que l'on avait renversé le sens des mots et leurs justes significations. *Marcher, déclamer, gesticuler*, était danser . . . Voilà donc le mot *danser* mis à la place de déclamer . . . Voilà encore le mot *chant* à la place de déclamer et celui de *danse* substitue à celui de *geste.*"

"I told you before that the meaning of words and their real signification was turned upside down. *To walk, to declaim, to gesticulate*, was to dance. . . So that the word *to dance* seemed to be standing for declamation. . . Then again the word *to sing* seemed to be interchangeable with the word *to declaim* and *dance* seemed interchangeable with *gesture.*"

Jean-Georges Noverre, *Letters sur la Danse et les Arts Imitateurs*, 1760.

I. Introduction.

A reverence from Fabritio Caroso's *Il Ballarino* (1581).

The courtly dance instruction books of Renaissance Italy, Burgundy and France have been dealt with in a variety of ways since they came to the attention of late nineteenth-century musicologists and theater historians. Still this wealth of material having been subjected to the scrutiny of two generations of reconstructors has yet to be examined as seminal for Western systems of kinetic theatricality.[1] A systematization or implicit theory of kinetic theatricality is extremely difficult to unravel because the dancing body in what has become classical theatrical dancing is both to all appearances arbitrarily codified (thus dance is a master category leading one to the assumption that a theory as such is possible for the body alone) and on occasion mimetic (beholden to Aristoltle's *Poetics*) though not necessarily both or either at the same time.

It should be borne in mind that my corpus of texts does not deal with the ballet de cour, the *masque* or the *mascarade.* The ballet de cour was a composite spectacle of the sixteenth and seventeenth century in France whose libretto called for the use of pantomime, declamation, decor, machines and costumes as well as dance. By contrast, the treatises we will study set forth the social dance which could be performed impromptu, *in camera* or in public. According to Ingrid Brainard, the first two real ballets or miniature dance dramas,"La mercanzia" and "la sobria," were written by Domenico da Piacenza between 1416 and 1425.[2] Representational or imitative social dance, however, constitutes the exception rather than the rule in the Renaissance. Although he does note that the *pavane* could be used in *mascarades*, Arbeau only speaks of imitation within a broad historical context when he makes reference to the Roman "saltations": ". . . aulcunefois on y adiouxte [à la danse] les masques pour monstrer les gestes d'un personnage que l'on veult representer." (". . . At one time masks were worn to accentuate the gestures of the character represented").[3] The distinction between social dance and mimesis reveals the pertinence of a theory of the former for an understanding of the early ballet spectacle.

Dance historians and reconstructors have on occasion called on social dance instruction manuals of the sixteenth century, chiefly the *Orchesographie,* for information applicable to the steps of the ballet de cour and the comédie-ballet. This practice is becoming increasingly questionable as we realize that while certain social dances were used in ballets, their employment was subsidiary to a new form: the geometrical dance. Among the social dances cited in mascarade descriptions around 1550 are to be found pavanes, courantes and branles. Arbeau notes that the pavane can be used in mascarades to herald the entrance of gods and goddesses and discusses the adaptability of the proto-dramatic structure of the courante to mascarades. Furthermore, certain branles such as the "Branle des Hermites," "de Malte," "des Sabots" as well as "les Canaries," according to Arbeau, were invented for given mascarades. Other isolated examples of the inclusion of social dance types into ballet de cour can be found in librettos. On occasion combat is choreographed by transforming cabrioles and gaillardes as in the *Ballet de Monseigneur le Duc de Vandosme* (1610). Very often mimetic movement revealing character is described as a kind of gait, an instruction on the borderline of acting and dancing. The character Fame in the *Mascarade du Triomphe de Diane* (before 1576) is said to walk "with such speed that one could think her foot didn't touch the floor, and that she was gliding on the tiles." Although the description is ostensibly of a walk, it seems highly likely that a form of the bourrée is at issue here, yet one more gliding than any found in Arbeau.

On the other hand, examples of social dance in ballet de cour can be found in which they are clearly felt to either need narrative justification or to be out of place within an altered vocabulary. For instance, in the libretto for the *Grand Bal de la Reine Marguerite* (1612), young girls dancing a branle are described as doing steps "more appropriate for a dance (bal) than a ballet." One of the reasons often given for creating a ballet in court was to surpass all others in every aspect of invention, including the invention of new steps. One cannot stress enough the extent to which known steps of the social dance repertory were improvised upon and transformed in ballets de cour.

I take the term theatricality, therefore, in its broadest sense, free of allusions to the theatrical conventions of dramaturgy, and yet also in its most radically primal sense as inseparable from the appearance of the human body and voice when inexplicably heightened and set into relief: theatricalized. The issue of theatricality as I would like to phrase it can appear at first to be a formalistic one, much as the well-known distinction between literarity and literality in criticism would sort out the specificity of the literary text through a notion of troping on a purely utilitarian language. For the dance the distinction has to be drawn between pedestrian and glorious uses of the body. Theatricality in social dance at this period, however, is rooted in ideology and in rhetorical strategies as well. To summarize, I am in search of the specificity of the dancing body at its inception in the Renaissance and am positing a fundamental physical theatricality as a point from which to understand theatricality in general.

My aim is to elaborate a working model for the relationship of the social dancer to his audience in the Italian and French Renaissance from about 1416 until 1589. In the fifteenth century the prominent texts are: Antonio Cornazano's *Libro dell'arte del danzare* (1455), Guglielmo Ebreo da Pesaro's *Trattato dell'arte del Ballo* (1455) and the untitled Paris manuscript of Giovanni Ambrosio (n.d.). I will also have occasion to compare and supplement these with the Paris manuscript of Domenico da Piacenza's *De arte saltandi et choreas ducendi* (c. 1416), the oldest of the four treatises.[4] These works deal initially with five or six "principles" of the dance. For Domenico they are "measure," "memory," "manner," "division of the terrain" and "air." Guglielmo Ebreo and Ambrosio add to those "body movement." For Cornasano they are "measure," "manner," "air," "diversity" and "division of the terrain." The treatises then proceed to describe choreography, broken down into three basic groups: the slow *bassadanze,* the livelier *balli* and the protodramatic *balletti.*[5]

The sixteenth-century text which will be of central importance to me is Thoinot Arbeau's *Orchesographie* (1588).[6] In the form of a dialogue between the master Arbeau and his student Capriol, this treatise begins as an apology of the dance and gradually progresses to an elucidation of the steps of the basse danse and the gaillard, as well as to shorter descriptions of many others. Choreography is either described in words or notated in letters (the *Réverence, branle, simple, double, reprise* and *congé* are notated as R, b, s, d, r and c respectively). The only symbolic notation in the Renaissance is to be found in the Cervera and Tarragó manuscripts.[7] It is not until 1700 that an autonomous sign language is elaborated by Feuillet in *Chorégraphie ou l'art de décrire la dance, par caractères, figures et signes démonstratifs.* I will deal only in passing with the Burgundian texts of the late fifteenth century because they offer less theory than the others. I should clarify immediately that by theory I do not mean that *practical* theory involved in the identification of a dance form or type by the limitations it imposes on the interpretation of a step, in the underlying order of the "mesures" (patterns of step groups) or in the breaking down of individual steps into a movement analysis. Nor do I mean by theory the universal key to step notation within a dance type. All dance manuals, to a greater or lesser degree, include this kind of theory whose concept is borrowed from and relies heavily on musical disciplines. The theory I am concerned with, on the contrary, is a *theoretical* one related to the esthetic of step execution: a systematic and generalizable perspective on movement quality within choreographic descriptions. Arbeau's notations have been considered far clearer and more detailed than those of the earlier Italian variety until the ground breaking work of Ingrid Brainard on fifteenth-century manuals. She nevertheless relies to some extent on late sixteenth-century Italian treatises as well as on Arbeau in order to elucidate ambiguous or absent step descriptions. Indeed, the corpus is complete if we take into consideration Fabritio Caroso's *Il Ballarino* (1581) and Cesare Negri's *Le Gratie d'Amore* (1602).

The inclusion of fifteenth-century Italian and sixteenth-century French texts in the same inquiry on the dancing body could be open to objections which I would now like to address. Between 1416 and 1589 three schools of dance are under consideration: the Italian school which encompasses the period from Domenico's 1416 treatise to Guglielmo Ebreo's work (1455); the Burgundian school which includes the "bal de la reine de cessile," otherwise known as the "Nancy basses danses" (1445) and the famous late fifteenth-century Brussels Basse dance manuscript; the French school is represented by the work of Michel Toulouze (c. 1486), Robert Copelande (1521), Antonius de Arena (c. 1528), the basses danses of Lyon published by Jacques Moderne (1530-38) and Thoinot Arbeau (1588).[8] The preeminence of the *bassadanza* and the basse danse is evident until 1550 in all of these regions and is Arbeau's centerpiece although he is clearly reviving it after almost forty years. Domenico called it the Queen of measures:

> Cio sono *bassadanza* de le mesure regina e merito di portar corona et in loperare de mi poche genti hano ragione e chi in danzare lo in sonare ben di me sadopra forza che da li cieli sia data lopra.[9]

> I am the *bassadanza* the Queen of measures and I deserve to wear the crown and in my execution few excel and he who can dance and play me well has been given a divine gift.

Clearly the *bassadanza* and the basse danse, despite the differences in choreography from region to region, is reducible to an identity which was exemplary for the Renaissance.[10] I have therefore chosen to focus my attention on a general movement theory of the *bassadanza* and basse danse.

The objection may be raised, however, that one is simply not speaking about the same dance when drawing on a corpus which extends from 1416 to 1589 and from Italy to France. What are the choreographic differences and to what degree do they reflect a changing technique? Ingrid Brainard has shown that the Nancy basses danses were influenced by the Italian *bassadanza,* indeed, were "stylistically at a midpoint between Brussels and Italy" as early as 1445.[11] She also affirms that the Brussels manuscript reveals a "direct Italian influence" and establishes the tripartite structure of the basse danse which recurs in Arbeau as current in the fifteenth century.[12]

Some American dance historian-reconstructors tend to eye Arbeau with diffidence as they measure his distance from the Italian and Burgundian schools when the basse danse enjoyed its heyday. Brainard considers Arbeau's version of the basse danse to be a decadent one.[13] It is rarely acknowledged that since Arbeau was born in Dijon in 1520 and died in Langres, where *Orchesographie* was published, in 1595, he was close to the Burgundian tradition and therefore to the Italian influence. It is nevertheless true that no comparable document on sixteenth-century Parisian court dance exists with which to compare Arbeau's "provincial" choreography. Certain French dance historians, on the other hand, appear to be assimilating Arbeau's choreography entirely to "danse populaire," thereby erasing dance as a courtly or court-derived and oriented phenomenon.[14] I might add that, although Italian dancing masters described court dances properly speaking while Arbeau wrote for the upper middle classes, this does not preclude the possibility of a common theory. In the elaboration of conduct and ceremony, a display of which the dance was certainly an integral part, the Renaissance was a period of models. For example, Erasmus' *De Civilitate Morum Puerilium,* while written in a relatively democratic spirit, played an important role in the inauguration of courtly conduct literature.[15] Moreover, all Italian courtesy books of note in the sixteenth century were either in polyglot editions or subsequently translated into French.[16] Perhaps a more reasonable inference than to posit an unbridgeable gap between Italian and French social dance would be to hypothesize an Italian influence passing into France through the Burgundian courts. As regards festivals, George Doutrepont writes that "par ses réunions fastueuses . . . la cour de Bourgogne semble annoncer les brillantes assemblées de la cour de France au XVIe siècle."[17] The Grand Bal which concluded banquets and entertainments was one of the major occasions for social dancing.

Two examples from the best available reconstruction work, that of Ingrid Brainard, will serve to illustrate why it is still impossible to isolate the Italian dance entirely from its northern neighbor and reconstruct its steps through an immanent reading. Brainard claims that the *doppio* with its full ornamentation reached its apogee in Cornazano's late fifteenth-century description and was subsequently on the decline from 1490 to 1581. Yet she can only derive the description of its ideal form from a Burgundian text.[18] She also derives what she considers adequate descriptions of the *posa* used by Domenico in 1416 from Arbeau.[19] Can one really posit a decadence as well as the perfect transmission of an untarnished tradition at one and the same time? These are not isolated examples. Brainard describes the fifteenth-century reverence for which there exist no explicit descriptions through those of Arena and Arbeau.[20] She explains the *frappamento* through Caroso (1581) and the *scambiamento* through Negri (1602) while she "deduces" the Italian *sempio* from the context of reconstructed dances. When all is said and done, if reconstructors must encompass a broader chronological spectrum of texts than they claim to do in order to produce a coherent reading there is no reason why the movement theorist, for whom there is substantially less textual data, should be deprived of the right to a similar procedure. I think it is healthy for scholars to admit that these exceptions to the avowed reconstructive method are symptomatic of a methodology that is not yet entirely scientific. The lack of textual data leads to a "flip-flop" logic in which the reconstructor's intuition acquires a pseudo-scientific basis: lacunae are filled with one of the following attitudes: 1) there is no reason to assume it is true; 2) there is no reason to assume it is *not* true. So, for example, while Brainard frequently resorts to French and Burgundian descriptions to elucidate Italian steps she eschews explaining the Italian *ripresa* by the Burgundian *reprise* since there is no Italian description. There is no reason, despite the homophony of the names, to assume they are similar. . . etc. By the same token, there is no reason to assume that fifteenth- and sixteenth-century physical dynamics in dancing are the same, but no reason to assume they are different either. I am obliged to extend my corpus for the same practical reasons that reconstructors are but in so doing I am making no claim to equate the *bassadanza* with the *basse danse* choreographically or even totally stylistically.[21] My working hypothesis is that a basic movement and postural theory of the *bassadanza* and the *basse danse* is retrievable and influences the subsequent development of physical theatricality in Western Europe down to this day. That the codified Renaissance dance step is an avatar of the "danse d'école" or classical ballet in the academic sense seems to me a modest hypothesis which hardly needs to be proved despite the stridently a-historical tone which proponents of the "bal folk" currently take in France when it comes to early dance. But despite all the parallels that could be drawn my study is not evolutionary but synchronic. It could, however, be considered as a prolegomenon to the ideology of classical ballet technique.

Dance treatises represent the first attempt in Western European culture to preserve dances in writing, as the title "Orchesographie" indicates: a writing ("graphie") of the *orchesis* or dance.[22] The object of my analysis is a practice which is transmitted to us and indeed only "subsists" as a text. Modern day reconstructions of Renaissance dances in their original form and style will always be a matter of conjecture based on different readings. Pervasive vagueness in technical terms and the frequently fragmented instructions contrast with numerous indications that the dance was a highly codified practice and create a gap between the text and the reality it was meant to represent. We may, in fact, reasonably ask whether treatises such as *Orchesographie* represent the dance of their day or whether they do not represent the thought of theorists, the cornerstone of a literary myth of dancing, or a utopian ideal of what the dance should have been. Arbeau explains to his student,

> On *dançoit* pavanes, basse-dances, branles et courantes: *les basses-dances sont hors d'usage depuis quarante ou cinquante ans*: Mais je prevoy que les matrones sages et modestes *les remettront en usage*, comme estant une sorte de dance pleine d'honneur et modestie.

> Our predecessors *danced* pavans, basse danses, branles and corantos: *the basse danse has been out of date some forty or fifty years*, but I foresee that wise and dignified matrons *will restore it to fashion* as being a type of dance full of virtue and decorum.[23]

For Arbeau, as for the modern reader and practitioner, dances were part of an almost mythical past to be conserved and fixed in writing.

If I raise the question of myth it is because beneath the one so familiar to the Renaissance of the cosmic dance lies another which also concerns the harmony of a universal consensus, that of a speaking body.[24] Apart from dance treatises themselves, Montaigne's long passage on body-language in the "Apologie de Raimond Sebond" may serve as an example.

> Quoy des sourcils? Quoy des espaules? Il n'est mouvement qui ne parle et un langage intelligible sans discipline et un langage publique: qui faict, voyant la varièté et usage distingué des autres, que cestuy cy doibt plus tost estre jugé le propre de l'humaine nature. Je laisse à part ce que particulierement la necessité en apprend soudain à ceux qui en ont besoing, et les alphabets des doigts et grammaires en gestes, et les sciences qui ne s'exercent et expriment que par iceux, et les nations que Pline dit n'avoir point d'autre langue.[25]

Accordingly, in the interests of a brand of allocution I will seek to delineate, dance treatises set forth the choreography of dances from the point of view of the dancer and the spectator. Failing a formal theatrical framework, the spectator should be understood by turns as being the partner and as any onlookers present. These two manners of observation correspond to the two models of my analysis: civility and rhetoric. Although the dance is often called a language, the effects of steps and movements in the communication of a message are not treated, nor is their possible sign value taken up. Nevertheless, the evolution of steps is meant to evoke admiration in the spectator. The dancer's own person is the ultimate and single object of praise or dispraise in the dance. The body is therefore also the instrument of effects on the spectator. Pierre Legendre has suggested that "il faut donc revenir à cette chose de base: le corps, tel qu'il est inventé par les procédures légalistes. Cette découverte n'est pas faite ou n'a jamais été faite historiquement, une fois pour toutes. Elle fonctionne en déclaration esthétique et par détournement du mythe au moyen de savoirs techniques."[26] However, the dancing body as such is barely a subject of treatises. As the dance scholar Rodocanachi put it, ". . . quant aux mouvements, c'est la danse en elle-même dont la connaissance semble avoir été la moindre des occupations du danseur.[27] We could also cite the earliest Italian treatises, mentioned above, in this regard. Among the five or six "principles" constituting the dance, "body movement," like oratorical action in the five departments of rhetoric, is the last and seemingly least important. This is as true for the Renaissance as for Aristotle, Cicero and Quintilian. Amyot, for example, explaining rhetoric as model for governing in his *Projet de l'Eloquence Royale* advises Henry the Third on the three domains of action: the voice, the face and gesture or "contenance." Gesture, however, comes up for discussion only to be summarily and inexplicably dismissed. "Quant a la bonne contenance, geste et mouvement du corps, ce seroit non seulement perte de temps et de papier mais aussi presomption, d'en vouloir ici toucher quelque chose." ("As for good demeanor, gesture and body movement, attempting to cover this subject would be not only a waste of time and paper but presumptuous as well").[28]

Quintilian was the only classical author to deal comprehensively with action and it was not until 1620 that some French treatises devoted exclusively to delivery were to appear.[29] Action was nevertheless essential to Renaissance eloquence as Rabelais' parody of its abuses suggests in the sign-language debate between Pantagruel and the Englishman.[30] Indeed, it was precisely the notion of a body-language perfectly transparent to the debators and just as opaque to the reader which Rabelais was deriding.

Between the anticipation of wondrous, indeed almost miraculous effects of "silent speech," of a "mute rhetoric," due to the myth of a body-language, and the classification of dances—including the laborious enumeration of a number of steps often of striking simplicity—the body is conspicuous by its absence. There is no connection between the effect and its technique of performance. Both lead separate existences, pursue separate paths. The dancing body is posited only in order to cede its place to a theory without an object.

An analogy with Michel Foucault's problematization of the absence of madness in the seventeenth and eighteenth centuries may be helpful in clarifying our problematic. Foucault localized the so-called absence of madness in the hiatus between its empirical perception and recognizability and its scientific classification.

> La maladie mentale, à l'âge classique, n'existe pas, si on entend par là
> la patrie naturelle de l'insensé, la médiation entre le fou qu'on perçoit et
> la démence qu'on analyse, bref le lien du fou à sa folie. Le fou et la folie
> sont étrangers l'un à l'autre; leur vérité à chacun est retenue, et comme
> confisquée en eux-mêmes.[31]

Similarly, there is no link in treatises between the body and its dance. I am
postulating an absence of the dancing body in dance treatises resulting from
the disparities between the theory of a body-language and the textual givens
of a language-body or a body written as a dance. The rules and precepts of
posture, the directives of choreography represent the body in language but
disarticulate the body from the "language of gesture." Treatises tell us to
some degree what to dance but not how to dance it. My aim is to uncover the
specificity of the dancing body as a movement quality or style of movement.

Certain misunderstandings may be avoided if one accepts the
distinction between choreographic movement and body movement which is
essential to my problematic. To my knowledge, no one has undertaken a
history of the dancing body as distinct from floor patterns and music. It is
only by focusing on the body per se that dance history and philosophy of
dance (for want of a better term) may be made to reinforce one another. To
the extent that the problem of the dancing body is addressed within the
context of choreography and music, it is usually treated as an afterthought.
For example, in Daniel Heartz's excellent article on the basse danse, while
he proves an evolution in the musical and choreographic structure of that
dance between 1450 and 1550, he asserts without futher ado that
performance technique underwent a parallel evolution.[32] However, to
conclude that the fifteenth century basse danse was "an extraordinarily
light and graceful" one merely on the basis of one quotation ("on va le plus
gracieusement que on peult"-"one moves as gracefully as one can") is to
ignore the need to analyze the notion of grace in the Renaissance. Likewise,
to claim that Arbeau's version of the basse danse became *pesante* because
of his desire that "les matrones sages et modestes" renew its popularity is to
misconstrue Arbeau's strategy of apologetics. Heartz writes of the French
sixteenth century: "What a far cry from the dance which Domenico of
Piacenza compared to the motion of a falcon!"[33] However, Domenico was
not evoking the falcon's flight as a mimesis of the basse danse but rather
delineating a physical dynamic within a binary opposition of movement and
stillness which created an esthetic of suspension I will discuss later (See
chapter IV,C).

What the dance signifies or reproduces is certainly not a discursive
aspect of the text's surface. Indeed, dance treatises engage on the one hand
upon an apologetic strategy saturated with humanistic erudition; on the

other they are dominated by questions of choreographic practice which tend to suffice unto themselves. The Polemical antidance treatises such as Simeon Zuccolo's *Pazzia del Ballo* (1549), Guillaume Paradin's *Le Blason des Danses* (1556), or Lambert Daneau's *Traite des Danses* (1582) contend that the dance is a form of vanity, passion or madness. Apologetics counter these attacks with a conception of the dance as a political and civil virtue, an object lesson in the then pervasive ideology of "la civilité nouvelle." Courtesy books will play a role in my analysis as a genre to be compared with Arbeau's quasi-speculative "definitions" or "theories" of the dance and the "principles" of Italian treatises. The model of intertextuality set up by Michael Riffaterre could be used to clarify the connections between dance treatises and courtesy books.

> . . . Two or more literary passages are collocable and comparable as text and intertext only if they are variants of the same structure. Intertextual connection takes place when the reader's attention is triggered . . . by intratextual anomalies—obscure wordings, phrasings that the context alone will not suffice to explain—in short, ungrammaticalities within the idiolectic norm (though not necessarily ungrammaticalities vis-a-vis the sociolect) which are traces left by the absent intertext, signs of an incompleteness to be completed elsewhere.[34]

The intertext, in Riffaterre's terms, is a presupposition or series of presuppositions compressed within a word or phrase and locatable in another text. In this case, the presupposition of *bienséance* (decorum) behind the signifier "danse" opens up a complex of rules for civil behavior directly marking civil demeanor as a semantic system for the dancing body, mediated by courtesy books. Riffaterre defines mediated intertextuality as the kind ". . . where the reference of text to intertext is effected through the intercession of a third text functioning as the interpretant that mediates between sign and object. . . "[35] A rhetorical intertext,—specifically that one which deals with oratorical action, Quintilian's *Institutio Oratoria,*—is the interpretant joining dance treatises to their intertext: courtesy books.[36] I will demonstrate this in two stages: first, inasmuch as the rhetorical intertext contains within itself reference to urbanity and thus furnished the deictic trace of a genre as intertext: courtesy books; secondly, inasmuch as the rhetorical code is actualized in a specific work, Stefano Guazzo's *La Civil Conversatione* (1574), enabling us to elaborate a model for the interaction of dancer and spectator, based on a strategy inherent to conversation.

I shall attempt to substantiate the intertextual connection between dance and civility in three stages. First of all through an examination of the myth of a body-language (Arbeau and Quintilian); secondly, through a sociological reading of courtesy books and a gymnastic treatise (Erasmus, Della Casa, Tuccaro), and finally through an analysis of the role of pedagogy in establishing the important distinction between movement and the pose as it relates to the basse danse and the gaillard. A model for the interaction between dancer and spectator based on conversation shall then be elaborated through a stylistic and structural analysis of parts of Guazzo's *Civil Conversatione*.

I should stress that I am concerned with the elaboration of a model indigenous to the representation of the dance in texts, be it referential or utopistic. In other terms, I am not attempting to escape the constraints imposed by my corpus in doing a positivistic reading. The theory and notation of dance in the Renaissance takes place and must be apprehended in a space of language and therefore through a close reading. To avoid confusion in the course of the following chapters, I will differentiate between two uses of the term code. Code, with a capital "C" taken to imply any written collection of laws, shall pertain to the conventions of the use of the body imposed by a society on the individual. Code with a lower case "c" shall refer to the convergence of descriptive systems which creates quasi-metaphorical rapports between two conventional sets of signs in the corpus. We shall see, for example, that the dance is set forth in a rhetorical code and civility in a financial one.

II. The Mythological Intertext: language

"De la façon non du langage."
("In the non way of language.")
Agrippa d'Aubigné, *Les Tragiques*, 1616

Two figures from Giovanni Battista Braccelli's *Bizzarie di varie figure* (1624)

A. *The Rhetorical code*

In order to investigate the myth that the dance is a language I will examine one of the most elaborate "definitions" of the dance from Thoinot Arbeau's *Orchesographie*.

> Mais principallement tous les doctes tiennent que la danse est une espece de Rhetorique muette, par laquelle l'Orateur peult, par ses mouvements, sans parler un seul mot, se faire entendre et persuader aux spectateurs, qu'il est gaillard digne d'estre loué, aymé et chery. N'est-ce pas à votre advis une oraison qu'il faict pour soy-mesme, par ses pieds propres, en gendre demonstratif?

> But above all, learned men maintain that the dance is a kind of mute rhetoric through which the Orator can, by his movements, without uttering a single word, make himself understood and persuade spectators that he is spirited [gaillard] and worthy of being praised, loved and cherished. Is it not in your opinion a discourse that he profers for himself, with his own feet, in a demonstrative genre?[1]

A rhetorical code is marked in this passage by the signifiers *Rhetorique muette* (mute rhetoric), *Orateur* (Orator), *persuader* (persuade), *oraison* (discourse) and *gendre demonstratif* (demonstrative genre). A mute rhetoric here is one in which the "orator" used action ("ses mouvements," "his movements") to the exclusion of words ("sans dire un seul mot,"— "without uttering a single word"). According to Quintilian each of the orator's hand gestures are independent of his posture: "The neck must be straight, not stiff or bent backward."[2] The orator's posture is the same as that of the dancer in the Renaissance:

> Our attitude should be upright, our feet level and a slight distance apart, or the left may be very slightly advanced. The knees should be upright, but not stiff, the shoulders relaxed, the face stern, but not sad, expressionless or languid: the arms should be held slightly away from the side. . .[3]

The orator's hand movements, however, are in no way those of the Renaissance dancer. Furthermore, the classical theory of oratorical action precludes the independence of gesture and discourse. Indeed, physical eloquence is based both on gesture (*gestus*) and delivery (*pronuntiatio*). Gesture traditionally encompasses bearing and carriage of the body as well as movement, while delivery refers to correct pronunciation as well as variations in tone: a kind of gestuality of the voice. Gesture, Quintilian informs us, ". . . conforms to the voice, and like it, obeys the impulse of the mind."[4] He further specifies that ". . . the movement of the hand should begin and end with the thought that is expressed."[5] Arbeau's text filters out a reading of mute rhetoric as oratorical action because the vocal element to which the classical theory of action subordinates gesture is missing. However, the semic selection of /persuasiveness/ and /communication/ for the vehicle of the rhetorical metaphor is evident on the surface of the text ("se faire entendre et persuader,"—"make himself understood and persuade").[6] The object of this persuasive communication is to move onlookers to praise and love the orator-dancer. Indeed, the term "loué" regenerates the rhetorical code in the following sentence, iterated and confirmed by the phrase "gendre demonstratif" (demonstrative genre). Among the three kinds of rhetoric enumerated by Aristotle in the "*Art*" *of Rhetoric,* the deliberative, the forensic and the epideictic, the demonstrative genre is synonymous with epideixis *(genus demonstrativum).* Epideictic oratory is the genre of praise and blame and its appropriate temporal framework is the present. Its topics are virtuous deeds *(gesta).* Epideixis is also the rhetorical genre of "art for art's sake," the demonstration of the orator's eloquence in and for itself. Aristotle:

> . . . the hearer must necessarily be either a mere spectator or a judge. . .
> For instance, a member of the general assembly is a judge of things to come; the dicast, of things past; *the mere spectator, of the ability of the speaker.* Therefore, there are necessarily three kinds of rhetorical speeches, deliberative, forensic and epideictic.[7]

Thus epideixis is concerned both with praise and with oratorical virtuosity. Dance consists in actions ("mouvements") which demonstrate something ("en gendre demonstratif") about the dancer who performs them ("pour soy-mesme," "for himself"). Furthermore, these movements are movements of self-praise or eliciting praise because they are epideictic as well as demonstrative. The dance can only be epideictic insofar as action is not dependent on thought in rhetorical theory. Otherwise, the "rapprochement" of "gendre demonstratif" and *genus demonstrativum* can only be considered a play on words. Within rhetoric itself there are ways in which action can be a form of persuasion independent of words or "the thought that is expressed."

For Aristotle, the function of rhetoric is ". . . to discover the real and apparent means of persuasion."[8] "Apparent" here signifies fallacious from a logical point of view, but such means are nevertheless admitted because rhetoric is concerned with appearance and the judge is a simple person.[9] Moreover, oratorical action is admitted by Aristotle under the auspices of the apparent. ". . . Since the whole business of Rhetoric is to influence

opinion, we must pay attention to it, not as being right, but necessary. . .
Everything . . . that is beside demonstration is superfluous; nevertheless, as
we have just said, it is of great importance owing to the corruption of the
hearer."[10] In a like manner, Aristotle distinguishes between two sorts of
persuasion: "Now, that which is persuasive is persuasive in reference to
someone, and is persuasive and convincing either at once and in and by
itself, or because it appears to be proved by propositions that are
convincing."[11] By extension, oratorical action is persuasive "at once and in
and by itself" because it is "beside demonstration." In this sense, physical
eloquence is the rhetoric of rhetoric, if we consider that rhetoric has always
been differentiated qualitatively from dialectic. Dialectic employs the
syllogism and rhetoric its abbreviated form, the enthymeme. In the
enthymeme one term of the syllogism is omitted or understood because
shared as probable, as part of the *doxa* common to speaker and listener.
Physical eloquence epitomizes the brevity of the enthymeme by omitting
or understanding *two* terms of the epideictic syllogism: [All orators who
speak well are glorious, I speak well], I am glorious. In other terms, there is a
way in which actions, like the enthymeme, can take the place of proof
although Quintilian does not clarify how it occurs. Sometimes it seems the
hands accomplish the proof: "As for the hands . . . it is scarcely possible to
describe the variety of their motions, since they are almost as expressive as
words . . . For other portions of the body merely help the speaker, whereas,
the hands may almost be said to speak."[12] At other times, the face is given
prominence: "by far the greatest influence is exercised by the glance . . . It is
this that inspires the hearer with affection or dislike, this that conveys a
world of meaning and is often more eloquent than all our words."[13] Then
again the whole body seems to accomplish the miracle: "The flanks must
conform to the gesture; for the motion of the entire body contributes to the
effect: indeed, Cicero holds that the body is more expressive than even the
hands."[14]

Although physical movement for Quintilian has all the prestige of
language,[15] he separates the practice of oratorical action from the symbo-
lization of meaning. " . . . I do not wish the gestures of oratory to be modelled
on those of the dance" he writes in book one.[16] This dictum is reiterated
more vigoroulsy in book eleven which specifically deals with gesture: " . . . The
orator should be as unlike a dancer as possible, and his gesture should
be adapted rather to his thought than to his actual words . . ."[17] If dance and
oratorical action are not equatable, in what sense does Quintilian's
explanation of epideixis offer a general theory of the effects of oratorical
action? Or, put in other terms, to what extent does the rhetorical code in
Arbeau point to a rhetorical intertext for the relationship of dancer to
audience in the Renaissance?

For Arbeau, the dance is epideictic insofar as it inspires the admiration for, and indeed love of, the dancer-orator in the present of his performance. If rhetoric is traditionally described as "the beautiful and fruitful union of reason and expression," mute rhetoric indicates that expression can act persuasively in the absence of reason.[18] Yet an "expressive" rather than verbal and rational notion of persuasion, although peripheral to rhetorical logic, can still be seen to link up with a concept of proof. Aristotle proposes three categories of proof: "the first depends upon the moral character of the speaker, the second upon putting the hearer into a certain frame of mind, the third upon the speech itself, in so far as it proves or seems to prove."[19] The first two categories of proof mentioned above may be carried out with extra-verbal means. "A conciliatory effect," writes Quintilian, "may be secured either by charm or style or by producing an impression of excellence of character, which is in some mysterious way clearly revealed both by voice and gesture."[20]

B. *Rhetorical Charm and Emotion as Urbanity.*

Rhetoric is not all natural for Quintilian because without artifice, charm and emotion would be impossible. "But since it is his [the orator's] duty to delight and move his audience . . . it becomes necessary for him to employ those additional aids which are granted to us by that same nature which gave us speech."[21] To charm and to move are the two effects which, while part and parcel of the mainstream rhetorical effort, may also most likely be achieved by extra-verbal or para-logical mechanisms such as action. In Quintilian the problem of eloquence as "art" or artificiality is always illustrated with reference to action or by theatrical example. The demonstrative genre is the most closely associated with effects of "art," *ostentatio,* display. "The term *epideictic,*" writes Quintilian, "seems to me to imply display rather than demonstration [" . . . non tam demonstrationis vim habere quam ostentationis"].[22] Epideixis, then, while naming a species of oratory, connotes a function of all oratory: ". . . while there are three kinds of oratory, all three devote themselves in part to the matter in hand, and in part to display."[23] The question of "art" in oratory is inseparable from one of the orator's chief general aims: to charm (*delectare*).[24]

Though common to all types of speeches, to charm is most properly the task of epideixis: " . . . There are three kinds of audience: one which comes simply for the sake of pleasure ["quod ad *delectationem* conveniat"], a second which meets to receive advice, a third to give judgement on causes."[25] It is with reference to the aim of charming that the resources of "art" come to the fore.

> And even if display is the object of declamation, surely we ought
> to unbend a little for the entertainment of our audience.[26] For even in
> those speeches which, although undoubtably to some extent concerned
> with the truth, are designed to charm the multitude ["ad popularem
> aptatae delectationem"] (such for instance as panegyrics and the
> oratory of display in all its branches) ["totumque hoc demonstrativum
> genus"] it is permissible to be more ornate and merely to disclose all the
> resources of our art, which in cases of law should as a rule be concealed,
> but actually to flaunt them ["ostentare"] before those who have been
> summoned to hear us.[27]

Charm has two techniques at its disposal: the figure (*elocutio*) and action.
Indeed, charm is at the basis of action's effectiveness: "There are three
qualities which delivery should possess. It should be conciliatory, persuasive
and moving, *and the possession of these three qualities involves charm as a
further requisite.* "[28]

In addition to charm and perhaps as an extension of it, Quintilian
describes the second aim of rhetoric, to move by arousing emotions. If
charm is conciliatory, emotion is persuasive because it carries with it " . . .
the power of assertion, which is sometimes more convincing even than
actual proof."[29]

> . . . It is this emotional power that dominates the court, it is this form of
> eloquence that is the queen of all . . . Proofs, it is true, may induce the
> judges to regard our case as superior to that of our opponent, but the
> appeal to the emotions will do more . . . For as soon as they begin to be
> angry, to feel favorably disposed, to hate or pity, they begin to take a
> personal interest in the case, and just as lovers are incapable of forming
> a reasoned judgement on the beauty of the object of their affections,
> because passion forestalls the sense of sight, so the judge, when
> overcome by his emotions, abandons all attempt to enquire into the
> truth of the arguments, is swept along by the tide of passion, and yields
> himself unquestioning to the torrent . . . Without this all else is bare and
> meagre, weak and devoid of charm ["ingrata"]. For it is in its power
> over the emotions that the life and soul of oratory is to be found.[30]

Arbeau's definition of the dance, which I will now cite in its entirety,
true to the rhetorical intertext, deploys an emotional series alongside of its
persuasive one. Just as the seme / persuasiveness / can now be seen to have
been generated *a posteriori* by proof of moral character (" . . . persuader aux
spectateurs qu'il est gaillard digne d'estre loué, aymé, et chery . . . une
oraison qu'il faict pour soy-mesme . . . " - "persuade spectators that he is
spirited and worthy of being praised, loved and cherished . . . a discourse

that he profers for himself . . ."), the seme /communicability/ is generated by Aristotle's second proof, favorably disposing the spectator, and expanded in terms of emotion.

> N'est-ce pas à vostre advis une oraison qu'il faict pour soy-mesme, par ses pieds propres, en gendre demonstratif? Ne dit il pas tacitement à sa maistresse (qui le regarde dancer honnestement et de bonne grâce) aymés-moy, desirés-moy? Et quant les masquarades y sont joinctes, elle ha efficace grande de mouvoir les affections tantost à cholere, tantost à pitie et commiseration, tantost à la hayne, tantost à l'amour. Comme nous lisons de la fille d'Herodias laquelle obtint ce qu'elle demanda au Roy Herode Antipe, aprés quelle eut dancé au banquet magnifique qu'il fit aux princes de son royaulme, a mesme jour qu'il estoit né. Comme aussi Roscius le faisoit bien paroistre à Ciceron, quant il adjançoit les gestes et actions muettes de telle façon, qu'au jugement de ceulx qui en estoient arbitres, il mouvoit aultant ou plus les spectateurs, que Ciceron eut peu faire par ses élocutions oratoires.

> Is it not in your opinion a discourse that he profers for himself, with his own feet, in a demonstrative genre? Does he not say tacitly to his mistress, who marks the seemliness and grace of his dancing, 'Love me. Desire me'? And, when miming is added, it has the power to stir emotions, now to anger, now to pity and commiseration, now to hate, now to love. Even as we read of the daughter of Herodias, who obtained her wish from Herod Antipas by dancing before him at the magnificent banquet he offered to the princes of his realm on his birthday. So it was also with Roscius, who proved to Cicero that by his employment of gesture and dumb show he could move the spectators, in the judgment of the arbiters, as much or more than Cicero had been able to by his eloquent orations.[31]

The command of love ("aymés-moy, desirés-moy" - "Love me. Desire me"), presented as the argument, substance or "statement of fact" of a mute rhetoric ("ne dit il pas tacitement" - "does he not say tacitly"), completes the rhetorical metaphor by proposing Aristotle's third proof, " . . . the speech itself, in so far as it proves or seems to prove," as a condensation of the first two. Indeed, if the dance is "a kind of" rhetoric, its argument or substance revolves around the persuasive pre-logical powers which promote the argument. The dance functions as an exordium and peroration of the proposition of persuasion itself.[32] The mention of masquerade, a spectacle difficult to define but which included the dance, permits a hyperbolic representation of emotion. The mask was not part of social dance as Arbeau describes it, but theatrical impersonation (prosopopeia) is an element of the appeal to emotions in rhetorical tradition. Quintilian writes, " . . . we may draw a parallel from the stage, where the actor's voice and delivery produce greater emotional effect when he is speaking in an assumed role than when he speaks in his own character.[33] The hyperbolic emotional series culminates in the example of Salome in which emotional appeal is reidentified with desire, and persuasiveness ("obtint ce qu'elle demanda" - "obtained her wish") is exercised by the act of dancing alone. The example of Roscius reinstates the text's expansion of emotion within the epideictic framework of judgement (" au jugement de ceulx qui en estoient arbitres" - "in the judgment of the arbiters"). The persuasive and emotional series are fused in that emotional power is itself judged persuasive. "Gestes et actions muettes" ("Gesture and dumb show"), iterating both the dance (*mute* rhetoric) and oratorical action ("gestes et actions" - "gesture" and "show"), are judged equal to and surpasssing the emotional appeals of eloquence by those who, under its effect, are by definition "incapable of forming a reasoned judgement."[34] The only reasoned judgement the spectator is able to form is the declaration that he is convinced and won over. The dance as a mute rhetoric requalifies "rhetoric," in Pascalian terms, as a tyranny. Indeed, for Pascal there was only one step from the "devoir d'amour à l'agrément" ("the binding of love to what is attractive") to the "devoir de crainte à la force" ("the binding of fear to force"). The progression from charm to emotion, in other terms from benevolence to love, from delectation to passion, suggests the rhetorical tyranny of the proposition: " 'Je suis beau, donc on doit me craindre. Je suis fort, donc on doit m'aimer . . . ' " (" 'I am beautiful, therefore I am to be feared. I am strong, therefore I am to be loved . . .' ").[35]

When Quintilian discusses the emotional force of impersonation in delivery, he makes a parallel between emotion and action which should help to clarify their relationship. "Actions as well as words may be employed to move the court to tears . . . It is with this in view that we see bloodstained swords, fragments of bone taken from the wound, and garments spotted with blood, displayed by the accusers, wounds stripped of their dressings, and scourged bodies *bared to view*."[36] Quintilian refrains from defining rhetoric as persuasion because there is a persuasiveness which does not rely on verbal eloquence, such as, " . . . some sight unsupported by language, when for instance the place of words is supplied by the memory of some individual's great deeds, by his lamentable appearance or the beauty of his person."[37] Such documentary evidence or the gestures which reveal it is allowed as a form of proof by Aristotle. I propose to pursue this form of proof with an eye to what it may reveal about the connection between action and emotion.

For Aristotle, although all proof is a demonstration,[38] some proofs are "demonstrative," others not. Demonstrative or "inartificial" proofs, which for Quintilian "lie outside of speaking,"[39] are inductions based on

. . decisions of previous courts, rumours, evidence extracted by torture, documents, oaths, and witnesses."[40] Artificial proofs, on the other hand, are deductions produced by the art of speaking or ethical argumentation. *Tekmeria,* for Aristotle, are inartificial proofs, "those which have not been furnished (i.e. invented) by ourselves but were already in existence."[41] They are then analytically true and need only be exhibited or enunciated. "Necessary signs are called *tekmeria* . . . for when people think that their arguments are irrefutable, they think that they are bringing forward a *tekmerion,* something as it were proved and concluded: for in the old language *tekmar* and *peras* have the same meaning (limit, conclusion)."[42] Aristotle gives the following example: " . . . if one were to say that it is a sign that a man is ill, because he has a fever, or that a woman has had a child because she has milk, this is a necessary sign. This alone among signs is a *tekmerion*; for only in this case, if the fact is true, is the argument irrefutable."[43] For Quintilian, the *tekmerion* is an indication of apodeictic certainty which he calls "signum" or "indicium." In the first place indications as a rule come under the head of inartificial proofs: for a bloodstained garment, a shriek, a dark blotch and the like are all evidence analogous to the documentary or oral evidence and rumours . . . "[44] What interests me is the element of display common to epideixis and to *tekmeria* which would enable us to grasp the link between emotion and action. The virtue of display is referred to by Quintilian as ἐνάργεια or *evidentia.* "Palpability [*evidentia*] . . . is no doubt a great virtue, when a truth requires not merely to be told, but to some extent obtruded [*ostendendum est*]."[45]

The relation of ἐνάργεια to epideixis, display or ostentation, is patent in Quintilian: "From such impressions arises that ἐνάργεια which Cicero calls *illumination* and *actuality,* which makes us seem not so much to narrate as to exhibit the actual scene, while our emotions will be no less actively stirred than if we were present at the actual occurrence."[46] The example of ἐνάργεια under discussion exemplifies display as a diacritical gesture which draws attention to the *tekmerion.* The actions Quintilian refers to are always those of showing, baring and unveiling. Demonstrative proof, like epideixis, implies display rather than logical demonstration.

With regard to action as display Quintilian allows that demonstrative gestures be used, as the exact equivalents of deictic speech utterances.

> I should, therefore, permit him [the orator] to direct his hand towards his body to indicate that he is speaking of himself, or to point it at some one else to whom he is alluding, together with other similar gestures which I need not mention. But on the other hand, I would not allow him to use his hands to imitate attitudes or to illustrate anything he may chance to say.[47]

In enumerating all that hands may be used to express or indicate, Quintilian offers one explicit reference to language: "do they [gestures] not take the place of adverbs and pronouns when we point at places and things?"[48] The pointing gesture is part of the Code of oratorical action.

Display then can be understood as a form of charm necessary to epideixis but also a form of deixis necessary to apodeixis. Demonstration can mean by turns logical argument, evidence and the act of showing. I do not mean to pack them all into the pharse "gendre demonstratif" in order to explain a mute rhetoric. I intend rather to isolate the sort of display which the demonstrative genre has in common with demonstrative proof.[49] To charm one's audience is to demonstrate one's ability by showing it. By the same token, Huguet informs us that *demonstrer* could have the same meaning as *monstrer* (to show) in the sixteenth century and supplies the following rhetorical example: "Licinius Regulus . . . deschira sa robe en plain senat, et . . . demonstra les cicatrices de ses playes"[50] ("Licinius Regulus . . . tore open his robe before the whole senate, and . . . showed [*demonstra*] the scars of his wounds"). One simply must imagine the orator as both demonstrator and demonstrated, displaying himself as evidence which provokes a favorable aesthetic verdict on the part of his audience, in order to comprehend what the dance as a demonstrative genre means. It is only if the verdict is reached instantaneously that display can be its own evidence and that a "gendre demonstratif" can connote apodeixis as well as epideixis.

A footnote of Curtius remarks on the division of the *genus demonstrativum* into panegyrical and epideictic oratory. "The term $\epsilon\pi\iota\delta\epsilon\iota\zeta\iota s$ (*ostentatio*) goes back to its aspect of display, the term $\pi\alpha\nu\dot{\eta}\gamma\mu\rho\iota\kappa o\varsigma$ to the outward occasion . . ."[51] Since the demonstrative genre is both a discourse of praise (panegyrical) and to be praised (epideictic), the dancing body must in turn display the admirable self for praise and index this display as praiseworthy, elicit praise. The dancer substitutes display for demonstration. He is both subject and object in an act of reflexive deixis.

But how can we apprehend an absolute closed system of irrefutable proof as a form rather than a content? How does the gesture of showing, baring, revealing a document of irrecusable authority in itself become a "documentary" gesture? It was the certitude of the orator which invested his gesture with emotional force. If Aristotle elaborated the logic of the *tekmerion*, Quintilian dwelled on its emotional presentation, its $\dot{\epsilon}\nu\dot{\alpha}\rho\gamma\epsilon\iota\alpha$. Emotion, for Quintilian, is not only associated with the apodeictic certainty of demonstrative proof in the instant of its realization. He qualifies ideal emotion as urbanity: " . . . a certain quality of language . . . adapted to delight and move men to every kind of emotion" ["adapta ad delectandos movendosque homines in omnem adfectum animi"].[52] Urbanity is " . . . the task of perfect eloquence . . . "[53] of which delight and emotion are the perfect effects. Quintilian divides emotion into two classes: "pathos" and "ethos." In "ethos" the force of emotion is distilled in charm:

> The one is called *pathos* by the Greeks and is rightly and correctly expressed in Latin by *adfectus* (emotion): the other is called *ethos,* a word for which in my opinion Latin has no equivalent: it is, however, rendered by *mores* (morals) . . . the former command and disturb, the latter persuade and induce a feeling of good will.[54]

Furthermore, charm is associated with both forms of prelogical proof enumerated by Aristotle: the favorable disposition of the audience and the orator's good character. Quintilian:

> The *ethos* which I have in mind and which I desiderate in an orator is commended to our approval by goodness more than aught else and is not merely calm and mild, but in most cases ingratiating and courteous and such as to excite pleasure and affection in our hearers . . . If *ethos* denotes moral character, our speech must necessarily be based on ethos when it is engaged in portraying such character . . . Finally *ethos* in all its forms requires the speaker to be a man of good character and courtesy.[55]

Quintilian shows that charm and emotion, like Aristotle's first two kinds of proof, are two sides of the same coin. Pleasure awakens admiration and admiration breeds affection. " . . . *Pathos* and *ethos* are sometimes of the same nature, differing only in degree; love for instance comes under the head of *pathos,* affection of *ethos* . . ."[56]

Action and emotion are articulated within the behaviorism of urbanity, that is, within the boundaries set by a given society for decorous behavior. The decorous, far from being ornamental, offers "documentary" proof of moral fiber.[57] Indeed, the noun *decor* in Quintilian sometimes means propriety and sometimes peculiar charm.[58] In order to pursue the full import of Arbeau's definition of the dance as a "mute rhetoric" for a model of the interaction of dancer and spectator I will turn to the outward manifestations of the Renaissance Code of propriety. The mythological intertext opens the way to a sociological one.

III. The Sociological Intertext: courtesy

" . . . En cecy [la danse] la Pratique et la Theorie doivent estre deux accidens inseparables."
" . . . In this [dancing] Practice and Theory must be two inseparable accidents."
François de Lauze, *Apologie de la Danse*, 1623

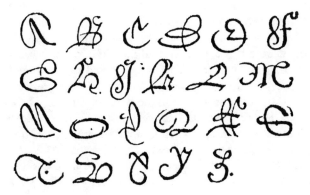

An alphabet from Claude Hours de Calviac's *La Civile Honestete* . . . (1560)

A. Dance as a theoretical practice of propriety: Tuccaro

There is one Renaissance text which relates dance to civility on a theoretical level.In the *Trois Dialogues de l'exercice de sauter et voltiger en l'air,* essentially a gymnastic treatise, Archange Tuccaro devotes the first of three dialogues to an apology of the dance.[1] Neither the apology nor the theoretical positions emanating from it are supplemented with practical examples of dancing. This is a theoretical text as far as dance is concerned. My discussion of it is meant merely to confirm, within the epistemological framework of the Renaissance, the relevance of a sociological intertext for the dancing body.

The dialogues unfold before the court of Charles the Ninth during a respite from the festive progess through Touraine celebrating his marriage with the Royne Elisabel. "Dans une grande sale, qui regardoit sur un jardin" ("In a large hall overlooking a garden"), the company is assembled to witness the leaps of the renowned gymnast Archange Tuccaro. Seigneur Cosme proposes that Tuccaro also expatiate on the " . . . reigles qu'on doit observer, par le moyen desquelles il s'est exercé à réduire en art et méthode, la vraye démonstration, et certaine conoissance de l'exercice du saut tourné en l'air . . . " (" . . . rules that must be observed, through which he went about reducing the true demonstration and certain knowledge of the exercise of the turning leap into an art and method . . . ")[2] Prior to Tuccaro's demonstration and pedagogical discourse, a debate unfolds in the meta-language of the etymological tradition. "Il suffit," says Cosme's inter-locutor Ferrand, "que la propriété des choses, mesmement des mots, se cognoisse, et s'entende selon la particulière signification qu'ils ont . . . " ("It suffices that the property of things, and in a like manner of words, be known and understood following the particular meaning they have . . .")[3] The crux of the debate is the etymological definition of the word *Palaestrita,* used by Cosme to predicate Tuccaro. Ferrand argues that *Palaestrita,* does not apply to Tuccaro because the term *Palestre* refers to the activity and place of wrestling as well as to the wrestler himself whereas Tuccaro is a master. He proposes the term *Palestricos* to predicate Tuccaro, " . . . d'autant que Afranius et Quintilian appellent *Palestricos,* les hommes qui sont desià maistres passez, et qui monstrent et enseignent cest exercice de la luicte . . . " (" . . . inasmuch as Afranius and Quintilian call *Palestricos* men who are already past masters and who show and teach martial arts . . .").[4]

Cosme maintains that *Palaestrita* is the appropriate term for the gymnast Tuccaro because it means "quelque sorte d'exercice que ce soit, soit du corps, soit aussi de l'esprit . . . il signifie aussi la profession de celuy qui reduit en art, en reigle et methode la vraye et parfaite cognoissance de sauter." ("any kind of exercise be it of the body or the mind ... it also means the profession of one who reduces the true and perfect knowledge of leaping into art, rule and method.").[5] Gymnastics is " ... le nom d'un art si universel, qu'il comprent touts les exercices du corps."(". . . the name of such a universal art that it encompasses all physical exercise").[6] The leap for Cosme is the transcendental signifier of exercise. Leaping is an exercise whose practice serves as a theory for all other exercise. Cosme illustrates the theoretical status of the gymnastic leap vis-à-vis other practices. " . . . Courir n'est autre chose, pour en parler à la verité, qu'un saut qui se fait de pas en pas l'un après l'autre alternativement continué, tantost sur un pied, et tantost sur l'autre ... Dont s'ensuit par necessité qu'on ne peut courir si on ne saute" ("Running is nothing else, to tell the truth, than a leap effected from step to step one after the other and continued in alternation . . . It therefore follows that one cannot run if one doesn't leap.")[7] Since the gymnastic leap is the "necessaire principe de tous les autres exercices" ("necessary principle of all other exercises"),[8] Cosme enumerates the "jeu de paume," equitation, and all other athletic acitvities even to the act of warfare itself as practical applications of leaping.

> De là vient que les assaults de villes sont ainsi appellez, non seulement pour le saut qui y est necessaire; mais pour signifier qu'il devroyent estre faicts, s'il estoit possible, en un saut, comme le nom d'assaut le demonstre. Que diray-je plus? le saut n'est pas seulement necessaire pour la chasse mais aussi pour l'escrime et le combat en duel; . . . Tellement que ceux qui ont la parfaite cognoissance d'un tel art, se peuvent dire à bon droict faire entière profession de la vertu, et toutes les nobles actions d'icelle.

> For that reason, the taking of cities are called "assaults,"[9] not only for the leap that is needed; but to signify that it should be done, if it were possible, in one bound, as the word "assault"reveals. What more is there to be said? Leaping is not only necessary for the hunt but also for fencing and dueling; . . . So that those who have a perfected knowledge of such an art can say with assurance that they are practicing virtue and all of its noble actions to the fullest.[10]

Ferrand counters that the movement of the leap is "naturellement contraire à l'homme . . . Le mouvement du corps de l'homme ne se devroit pas appeller naturel, qui toujours s'encline, et tend en bas; ains plustost forcé et violent" ("naturally contrary to man ... Man's bodily movement shouldn't be called natural, when it starts with a downward motion in a forced and fairly violent way.")[11] So begins a polemical debate on the dance whose parameters are essential versus accidental movement.

Ferrand proposes the exercise of dancing as a theoretical activity of greater extension because "chorea" or "saltatio" comprise ". . . plusieurs especes, et differences de sauts qui ne servent, ny à la santé, ny au service de la guerre" (". . . several kinds and classes of leap which are useful neither for health nor for warfare.")[12] Ferrand undertakes a systematic defense of the dance by distinguishing the dancing leap from the gymnastic one. "Il faut donc remarquer que de ce verbe latin *Salto, Saltas,* qui proprement pris signifie baler, fut formé ce nom *Saltator,* qui signifie baladin; et non pas du verbe *Salio, Salis,* lequel emporte la vraye signification de sauter proprement, comme fait fort bien notre S. Archange . . . " ("We should observe that from this Latin verb *Salto, Saltas,* which properly means to dance, the word *Saltator* was formed which means dancer; and these terms don't derive from the verb *Salio, Salis,* which contains the true meaning of leaping properly speaking, such as our S. Archange does so well . . . ")[13] Ferrand blurs the etymological distinction with reference to usage: " . . . Et bien que plusieurs s'en servent souvent sans prendre garde de si pres à ceste differente proprieté; si ne me souvient-il point avoir leu qu'aucun aye usé du mot *Saltatio,* pour denoter le bal ou la dance" (" . . . And although some people use these terms interchangeably without being particular about their properties, I don't remember reading that anyone ever used the word *Saltatio* to denote the ball or the dance.")[14] The Latin noun "saltatio" is polysemous, referring both to gymnastics and to dance. Ferrand proposes a division of leaping in four categories which exploits this polysemy. The first category of leaping is the gymnastic leap " . . . par le moyen de laquelle on ne peut apprendre ny remarquer autre chose qu'une disposition et force acquise par ces exercices, pour rendre le corps plus agile et dispos, et en temps de paix, et en temps de guerre" (" . . . through which one can only learn and observe a readiness and strength acquired from these exercises which render the body agile and alert in times of peace and war.").[15] The next three categories relate the noun "saltatio" to the verb "saltare." It is the first of these three, however, which Ferrand would defend as the ideal dance.

> . . . Je dis que l'art de la dance et du bal, suivant les termes et preceptes de la modestie et honnesteté civile . . . est la premiere des trois susdites especes comprises sous la generalité du nom *Saltatio,* ou du saut. La qualité et usage de ceste espece est celle que j'entends louer, et defendre contre toutes les calomnies. . .

... I say that the art of the dance and the ball, in accordance with the terms and precepts of modesty and honorable civility ... is the first of the three above mentioned species included in the general term *Saltatio,* or leaping. The quality or use of this kind is the one I shall praise and defend against all calumnies.[16]

The ideal dance proposed by Ferrand is a hybrid of the gymnastic and the dancing leap. Just as Ferrand claims that in common usage "saltatio" denotes the gymnastic leap, the first category of the dance, "salto," participates in the meaning of "salio."

... D'autant qu'on ne trouvera jamais que l'exercice, et pratique de ceste-cy que je mets pour une espece, suivant la generale signification de *Salto, Saltas,* pris mesme pour signifier le viril exercice de sauter sans chansons melodieuses, ou musicales, et pour mesme signification que denote simplement ce verbe Latin *Salio,* aye jamais esté blasmee ...

... No one has ever blamed this last exercise and practice that I have designated as a species, following the general meaning of *Salto, Saltas,* taken also to signify the virile exercise of leaping without melodious and musical songs, and for the same signification as the Latin verb *Salio* simply denotes. . .[17]

All representational functions of the dance fall into the next category which is to be avoided:

La troisieme espece ... est accompagnee des mouvements et gestes du visage, et autres membres du corps, et qui imite la parole, et le maintien non pas seulement des hommes, et des femmes, mais aussi des animaux irraisonables... et c'est ceste espece du bal et de la dance que toutes les Republiques, dites vous, ont blasmee, et condamnee, et quelquefois bannie et reputee vile, infame, et indigne des hommes vertueux.

The third kind ... is accompanied by movements and gestures of the face and other members of the body, and imitates the words and attitudes not only of men and women but also of animals deprived of reason ... and it is this kind of ball and dance that all Republics, you say, have blamed and reputed to be vile, infamous and unworthy of virtuous men.[18]

Ferrand defends the ideal dance as against the mimetic. The ideal dance excludes imitation inasmuch as it shows a "theory-in-act," the adequation of movements with the image of their own principles. That is to say, if the practice of the ideal dance is meant to "represent" anything, that object to be represented would be its own theory. Furthermore, by combining his first category with a third, Ferrand modifies his theory with a notion of practice upon which the theory can operate. The fourth kind of leap, or third kind of dance, according to Ferrand, is the popular dance of the time:

> . . . laquelle j'entends consister en l'usage de sauter et baller, qu'on voit aujourd'huy observer en plusieurs provinces, mesmes entre personnages Plebeïens, sans observation des temps, proportions et mesures que les hommes ont par le moyen de l'Art de Musique inventé peu à peu, les faisant tomber en accord ensemblement, n'estant mis en doute ce qu'un chacun sçait, et peut naturellement faire plusieurs et divers sauts sans aucun aide, ny observation des reigles et proportions, ou preceptes de l'art . . .

> . . . which consists in jumping and dancing, such as can be seen today in several provinces, even among plebians, without observing tempo, proportion or measure which men invented gradually to keep them together, so that no one is concerned with ability and all can do a variety of leaps without paying attention to rules and proportion or the precepts of art . . .[19]

This last category of dance represents an undiscerning or primitive activity which must be modeled by art or "measure": "Mais l'art a esté adjousté pour disposer et reigler le mouvement de nostre corps avec quelque grace plus grande que celle que nous ministre la nature" ("Art has been added to arrange and regulate our body movement with a greater grace than nature alone can give us.").[20] The realization of an ideal dance comes about in the · fusion of categories two and four: the synthesis of " . . . la bienseance des honnestes mouvements, gestes, façons, formes, postures, et actes . . . de tout le corps ensemble . . . " (" . . . the decorum of honorable movements, gestures, ways, forms, postures and acts . . . of the whole body together . . ."),[21] with " . . . le mouvement qui est un effet naturel en nous . . ." (" . . . the movement which we possess naturally . . .").[22]

It now becomes evident that "Palaestritas," if it is not the proper term for the gymnastic master, is the proper term for the dancing master. Ferrand calls "Palaestritas" those who "en l'instruction de ceste bien-seance du mouvement du corps, sont excellement bien expers et exercitez" ("in the instruction of that decorum of body movement are well exercised and expert").[23] Ferrand qualifies the performance of the dancing master in these terms: "Et m'asseure que si vous avez jamais veu le comportement d'un maistre baladin, que vous n'aurez remarqué en son eschole qui ne semble *directement viser au but de la vertu* . . ." ("I am certain that if you have ever seen the behavior of a dancing master you have observed nothing in his school which does not *aim directly at the ends of virtue . . .").* [24] Dance is said to be the principial exercise of the body's propriety just as the gymnastic leap contains the theory of its athleticism. The institutionalization of a social dance in the sixteenth century is legalized with reference to "bien-séance" (decorum), the practice of good manners. One can envisage the sobriety of the French dance not as a decadent Italian form having rigidified but rather as the result of a strict separation of the functions of imitation from formal dancing. The vehicle of "bienséance," its product as a model and its model as an ideal product, is the body.

B. *The reverence as an aleatory intertext*

A series of parallels between dance and civility come to mind when we read that Arbeau's student Capriol calls the dance a civility: "Mectez en [de la danse] quelque chose par escript cela sera cause que j'apprendray ceste civilité" ("Set these things down in writing to enable me to learn this civility").[25] It should therefore be useful to refer to Michael Riffaterre's distinction between two sorts of intertextuality: the aleatory and the obligatory. The process of reading implied by the procedures of mediated intertextuality which I described earlier is an example of obligatory intertextuality. Without it we would remain on the level of generalities. The aleatory intertext is suggested by a kind of free association triggered by our memory of other texts.[26] I will not dismiss the aleatory intertext upon which all commentaries of Renaissance dance have been founded without first exploiting it to show the way the dance was an ideological extension of civility. In my opinion, the ideological connection has never been adequately explained. The reverence will provide my chief example.

Before the professionalization and ethnicization of the dance, didactic literature on social behavior acted as a text of reference for all social acts. The physical discipline required by the dance was in many ways indistinguishable from that required by civility. The Renaissance dance step was not yet the "established unit of motion"[27] of the academic classical ballet or "danse d'école" whose forms may be traced from the eighteenth to the twentieth century. Perhaps this is because physical training was only formalized in the Renaissance within the social context and not on the technically systematic level of dancing skills. Instructions for the position of the feet while standing, for example, are the same in dance treatises and courtesy books. Arbeau details two basic positions or "contenances" for standing: "pieds joincts" (joined feet), and "pieds largyz" (feet and legs apart). He adds to both the possibility of keeping the feet straight ahead, or of turning them out, away from each other, which he calls "une obliquité." "Et si d'avanture l'une des semelles demeure directement posée pour sobztenir seulle la pesanteur du corps, et le tallon de l'aultre pied se joinct à icelle, et torne l'arteil obliquement: Cest contenance sera appelle pied joincts oblique . . ." ("And if it happens that one foot is so placed as to support the whole weight of the body and the heel of the other foot is brought close to it with the toe at an oblique angle, this pose will be called *pieds joincts oblique . . .*")[28] When Capriol asks which position he prefers, Arbeau responds:

Pieds largyz   Pieds ioinɛts

Pied ioinɛt obli-   Pied ioinɛt obli-
que droiɛt   que gaulche

Illustrations from Thoinot Arbeau's *Orchesographie* (1588).

l'une de celles qui ont le pied oblique me semble plus belle, car nous voyons ès medalles et statues antiques, que les Monopedes sont treuvés plus artistes et plus aggreables. Et quand aux pieds joincts ou aux pieds eslargis directement, ils sentent leur contenance foeminine: Et tout ainsi qu'il est mal-seant à une Damoiselle d'avoir une contenance hommace, aussi doibt l'homme eviter les gestes muliebres . . .

One of those in which the foot rests at an oblique angle would appear to me the most beautiful, because we observe in ancient medals and statues that figures resting upon one foot are more artistic and pleasing. As for feet close together, or toes too positively turned out, these have a feminine appearance. And in the same way that it ill becomes a damsel to assume a masculine bearing so we should avoid feminine poses.[29]

These same directions are essentially reproduced almost a hundred years later in the chapter "des pieds" of *Le Nouveau Traité de la Civilité qui se pratique en France parmi les honnêtes gens.* "Demande. Estant debout, comment tiendra-t-il les pieds? Réponse. Il les tiendra tournés à demi en dehors, les deux talons separés environ de quatre doigts" ("Question. When standing, how will he keep his feet? Answer. He will keep them turned out by half, the two heels separated by about four fingers").[30]

"It cannot be repeated enough," writes Françoise de Ménil, "that the history of dance is the history of manners."[31] The intertextuality of civility is suggested by historical dance scholarship. "It seems," writes John Schikowski, "that at that time one didn't take pleasure in dancing, as if one didn't want to express one's feelings and moods in the release of animated rhythmic body movement. The end of the dance was rather directed to the exhibition of one's own person. The effort of he who danced was to show dignity, gracefulness and the exact knowledge of rules of decorum and propriety."[32] Schikowski is describing an overlapping of Codes in the formalization of two practices. Good dancing is concommitant to social success. Bad dancing is a breach of etiquette. Rodocanachi outlines some details of Code overlapping. "'Qu'elles sachent sauter afin qu'on ne dise point qu'elles soient dépourvues d'intelligence,' écrivait Barberino au XIVe siècle dans son traité sur les femmes" ("'Let them know how to leap so that no one takes them for unintelligent' wrote Barberino in his fourteenth-century treatise on women").[33] When Arbeau makes reference to Atheneus as one of the repositories of the techniques of dance and a source of its apology, the same confluence of Codes is implicit. "Voyant danser gauchement Hippoclide d'Athènes, un de ceux qui prétendaient à la main de sa fille, il dit aussitôt: 'Clisthène a *dédansé* son mariage.' Il pensait probablement que l'âme d'Hippoclide était conforme à sa manière de danser" ("Seeing one of his daughter's suitors, Hippoclide of Athens, dancing awkwardly, he said immediately: 'Clisthene has *undanced* his marriage.' He probably thought that Clisthene's soul conformed to his manner of dancing").[34] Dancing is that formalization of the civil act which makes the act no longer an index of manners but a predicable. One might say that the dance in the Renaissnace transforms conventional properties into essential ones.

But within the discourse of "savoir vivre," civility is not equated with dance. We read in *Le Nouveau Traité*: "D. En marchant quels defauts evitera-t-il touchant les pieds? . . R. Il ne marchera point sur la pointe des pieds, en dansant . . ." ("Q. In walking what faults will he avoid concerning the feet?. . A. He will not walk by dancing on the tips of his toes . . .").[35] In the eighteenth century Baudoin still sets strict limits to the use of dance in civility.

> 1° Je placerois la danse dès les premières années de l'éducation, afin d'accoutumer un jeune Seigneur à marcher de bonne grâce; et à se bien tenir sur ses pieds; à faire la révérence avec décence, et àvoir un air libre, naturel et dégagé. 2° A mesure qu'il avanceroit en âge, je ne lui laisserois apprendre que les danses les plus simples . . . les plus propres à former le corps et la taille, qui est la principale fin de cet exercice.

> 1° I would put dance into the early formative years to accustom a young Gentleman to walk with grace; to stand correctly on his feet; to do the reverence decently and to seem free, natural and unconcerned. 2° As he advances in years I would only let him learn the simplest dances . . . those that are most suited to develop his body and waist, which is the principal aim of this exercise.[36]

Arbeau adds a sexual dimension to the ends of the dance: "elle se treuve necessaire pour bien ordonner une societe" ("it becomes an essential in a well ordered society"). In a ritual of courtship, the presuppositions of dance as an exercise are contradicted by the attainment of a result: ". . . *Car les dances sont practiquées pour cognoistre si les amoureux sont sains et dispos de leurs membres*, à la fin desquelles il leur est permis de baiser leurs maistresses . . ." (". . . *Dancing is practiced to reveal whether lovers are in good health and sound of limb,* after which they are permitted to kiss their mistresses . . .").[37] We know from Montaigne that the kiss was part of the French reverence. "C'est une desplaisante coustume, et injurieuse aux dames, d'avoir à prester leurs lévres à quiconque a trois valets à sa suite, pour mal plaisant qu'il soit" ("It is a disagreeable custom, and unfair to the ladies, to have to lend their lips to any man who has three footmen at his heels, however unattractive he may be").[38] Although the kiss in itself cannot be danced and adds nothing to our grasp of the specificity of the dancing body, a study of the reverence reveals the most interesting parallels between civility and dance.

Reuerence

The following passage from *Orchesographie* on the manner to behave at a ball is quoted by de Menil as proof of " . . . the fortunate influence that dance had on manners."[39]

> . . . Quand vous seres entré au lieu ou est la compagnie préparée pour la danse, vous choisirés quelque honneste damoiselle, telle que bon vous semblera, et ostant le chapeau ou bonnet de vostre main gaulche, lui tendres la main droite pour la mener danser. Elle, sage et bien apprise, vous tendra sa main gaulche et se lèvera pour vous suyvre.

> . . . When you have entered the place where the company is assembled for the dance you will choose some comely damsel who takes your fancy, and, removing your hat or bonnet with your left hand, proffer her your right to lead her out to dance. She, being sensible and well brought up, will offer you her left hand and arise to accompany you.[40]

There is no appreciable difference between the movements described in this reverence of 1588 and Erasmus' description of one in 1530 from the chapter "de Concressibus" ("of Meeting") in *De Civilitate Morum Puerilium.*

> Si quis occurrit in via, vel sento venerandus, vel religione reverendus, vel dignitate gravis, vel alioqui dignus honore, meminerit puer de via decedere, reverenter aperire caput, non nihil etiam flexis poplitibus.

> If a child passes someone on his way to whom respect is owed either through respect for his age or reverence for his religious rank or other honor, he should step aside, remove any hat and even bend his knees a little.[41]

Nor do the movements vary in Calviac's description of 1560:

Il y a plusieurs façons de faire la reverence, selon les pays ou on se trouve et les coustumes d'iceux: Mais les francoys, ployent seulement le genouil droyt se tenans autrement plustost droyctz que enclines, avec un doux contournement et mouvement du corps: et ostans le bonet de la main droyte le tenant ouvert par le dedans l'abaissent au mesme costé droyt.

There are several ways to do a reverence depending on which country one is in and its customs: The French hold themselves more straight than bent forward and bend only the right knee with a soft twisting and movement of the body: and removing the hat with the right hand and holding it open from the inside they lower it on that same right side.[42]

Indeed, in the degree to which a Code of dancing and of civility intersect, courtesy books offer a greater wealth of descriptive detail than dance treatises.

However, in everyday life, the reverence may be symbolic of honor and respect and marks social hierarchies. "All reverences," writes Karl Heinz Taubert, "originally had a religious meaning; they signified subordination to the power of God. Only later did they signify subordination of a worldly order, subsequently to become a generalized form of greeting."[43] This point of view is borne out by Della Casa's satirical picture of the evolution of ceremony:

... Quelle solennità che i cherici usano d'intorno agli altari e negli uficii divini e verso Dio e verso le cose sacre si chiamano propriamente cirimonie; ma, poiché gli uomini cominciaron da principio a riverire l'un l'altro con artificiosi modi fuori des convenevole ed a chiamarsi padroni e signori tra loro, inchinandosi e storcendosi e piegendosi in segno di riverenza ... fu alcuno che non avendo questa nuova e stolta usanza ancora nome, la chiamò cirimonia ...

... those solemnities that churche men doe use at their Altars, and in their divine service bothe to God and his holy things, are properly called *Ceremonies:* but after, men did begin, to reverence eche other with curious entertaynements, more then were convenient, and would be called masters and Lords, amongst themselves, yealding bending, and bowing their bodyes, in token of reverence one to another ...and finding these newe founde curious follyes without any name: thought good to Christen and call them *Ceremonies* ...[44]

Taubert also notes that the French derived the term "révérence extérieure" from the Latin "reverentia" ("tribute"). The reverence was an act recognizing glory and reputation by a humbling, literally a lowering, of one's own body. As a form of greeting between equals, the reverence is an expression of affability.

De Ménil does not remark that the reverence in *Orchesographie* is an integral part of dances themselves: "La reverence premier geste et mouvement, tient quatre battements de tabourin qui accompaignent quatre mesures de la chanson que sonne la flute" ("The reverence, the first gesture and movement, occupies four tabor rhythms accompained by four bars of the tune on the flute").[45] In the danced reverence, as opposed to its "civil" enactment, the only distinction made is a sexual one. The reverence is the first movement of the basse danse and the gaillard. It is also a gesture which opens conversation. As an instance of the interimplication of civility and dance, the reverence could be described in two complementary ways: in dance it mimics behavior; as behavior it seems choreographed. During the social greeting conversation is danced: the modalities of dance and conversation are for a brief moment identical. Similarly, the reverence when performed to music suggests that the dance is a vast metaphor for conversation.

The double role of the reverence can be explained sociologically. Dancing served two purposes for the noble. First of all, it was a formative exercise through which he or she could master the physical requirements of social life. Dancing was, in this sense, an abstract civility, a practice of the theory of a practice. On the other hand, dancing was also a societal recreation in which expertise was a highly regarded accomplishment, no longer an exercise to an end but an end in itself. In this second sense, dancing was a ritual abstraction rather than an analytical one. As an exercise dancing served a pedagogical and initiatory function since it was part of a pedagogical tradition which transmitted the social Code. As a ritual dancing served a synthetic and mystificatory function: the "bal" provided an occasion for the body (and the voice when songs were sung as accompaniment) to perform unfettered by verbal content and the physical limitations of given situations. "M. de Nemours," writes Mme. de Lafayette, " . . . passait *par-dessus* quelques sièges pour arriver où l'on dansait" ("M. de Nemours passed over several chairs to arrive on the dance floor").[46] If the text tells us that Nemours practically flies over furniture to reach the dance floor, it does so not as a mimesis of acceptable social behavior but as a semiosis of the elimination of concrete obstacles to physical performance. Books on children's etiquette provide an intertext for the dance as a formative exercise. The "arts de plaire" furnish an intertext for the dance as an effect on the social group in conversation.

C. *The Courtesy Book as a Genre*

Civilitas is a term whose meaning crystallized between 1525 and
1550 after the publication and translation of Erasmus' *De Civilitate
Morum Puerilium*. Writings on civility are usually divided into two basic
categories: manuals for children and the "arts de plaire" or "Courtisans."[47]
The content of children's manuals is inseparable from their pedagogical
strategy: to inculcate the "rudiments" of virtue as the mechanical reproduction
of its appearance or signs. It is important to note that virtue in courtesy
books is "defined" in two ways. It may be defined tautologically as
techniques for the production of its appearance. The technical term for
virtue in both civility and dance is measure. Virtue may also be defined
negatively as the avoidance of its contrary. This definition is equally
circular. In this case again, being virtuous and acting appropriately are one
and the same. Quintilian's definition of urbanity is a case in point. " . . .
Urbanity involves the total absence of all that is incongruous, coarse,
unpolished and exotic whether in thought, language, voice or gesture . . ."[48]
This double bind will have consequences for the representation of the body.

The text of precepts is an object-lesson. Printed for the most part in a
script known as civilité type, they served as primers for exercises in
penmanship and reading. The first manual to be printed in civilité type,
Granjon's *La Discipline et institution des enfans* of 1558, blended
characteristically the apprenticeship of morals, manners and penmanship.

> So that youth aspiring to virtue and studying to acquire the manners
> suited to its years may have a twofold profit from this instruction in La
> Civilité puérile (gentle reader), I put it before you in the French
> character, proper only for our mother tongue believing that *children
> may benefit not only from that instruction but from the letters too,* as
> being the writing proper to their language and not borrowed from
> another people.[49]

The child was called upon to reproduce, to "recite" vocally and scripturally,
the letter of the text while the content of the text instructed him in the vocal
and physical reproduction of the forms of virtue.[50] Precepts of the voice
concern diction exclusively. Good diction involves the modulation of tone,
the avoidance of regional accents and an even rhythm in delivery. Physical
demeanor consists in bodily erectness and symmetry as well as the balance
of all physical attitudes between two extremes. One extreme is excessive
agitation and the other is motionlessness:

In questo anco vi si richiede un tal temperamento, che l'huomo col poco
non rappresenti l'immobilità delle statue, e col troppo l'instabilità delle
simie.

In this such moderation is required that a man with too little may be
immobile like a statue and with too much as unstable as a monkey.[51]

While precepts favor relative immobility, absolute motionlessness is as
much a vice as excessive movement because it is a sign of sloth:

... Veu qu'il est tres-certain que si nous ostons de l'esprit ou du corps
l'exercice, on n'y peut rien laisser en son lieu; on n'y peut substituer,
mettre ou faire de necessité succeder autre chose que la seule oisiveté
de tous reputee abominable ...

... Since it is certain that if we remove exercise from the mind or the
body, nothing can be put in its place; one can substitute nothing for it or
replace it with anything but idleness which all hold to be abominable.[52]

Virtue itself is usually described as measure, i.e. at once the "moderation"
of the mean between two extremes and order (the appropriateness of time
and place for an action). Lack of measure is a grave fault.

... et ce defaut provient du desordre et du peu de reigle, et mesure qu'il
y a aux actions des hommes. Il faudroit que ce desir fut borné et limité
par la raison, et contenu aux termes de la vertu qui gist entre ces deux
extremes, le trop, et le trop peu. C'est ceste voye du milieu, auquel nous
devons adresser non seulement nos desirs, mais aussi toutes nos
operations, paroles et actions.

... and this fault results from the disorder and lack of rule and measure
in men's actions. This desire must be limited by reason and contained
within the boundaries of virtue lying between the extremes of too much
and too little. It is to this middle road that we should address not only all
of our desires but also all of our doings, words and actions.[53]

Measure as order also justifies the arbitrariness of precepts by making them
prerequisites for both moral and intellectual perfection. In the *Fior di Virtu*
good posture is concommitant to the proper ordering of discourse.

Elqntodecimo e ultimo vitio e a non sapere di sponere per ordine quello
che lhuomo vuol dire. Et per tanto prima debbe ordinare e ben
disponere la sua persona: cioe che la sua faccia sempre sia dritta: et li
suoi labri non torcha niente: el guardo d gliocchi no tengha sempre

fermo contro a coloro alliquali parla, ne troppo inclinata in terra: ma
con qualche temperamento di bella maniera, si come siconvience, piu
conforme che sia possibile alle parole che lui vuol dire: ne non muova la
testa, ne lespalle, ne le mani, ne i piedi, ne alchuna parte della sua
persona: et guardisi di sputare o di forbirsi el naso quanto puo.

Fifteenth and last. This is when a man is incapable of putting in order
that which he wants to say. First of all he must arrange and place his
person in an appropriate manner. This means that his face must always
be straight, and he must not twist his lips. He should not keep his eyes
fixed on the ground. But he must deport himself graciously as the
situation requires, conforming his expression as much as possible to
that which he plans to say. Nor should he move his head, nor his
shoulders, nor his hands, nor his feet, nor any part of his body. Never
spit nor pull up with his nose, if he can help it.[54]

Just as virtue is constitutionally a boundary, limit or mean between
passionate extremes, civility deals, as Norbert Elias has pointed out, in a
principle of constraint. "Civility is based on self-imposed constraints which
have become automatic."[55] An illusion of surveillance is maintained at all
levels of privacy and sociability. Thus precepts are not merely suggestions,
they are imperatives which impose a discipline on each moment of one's
existence. While some precepts seem dictated by the requirements of a
particular decor, i.e. at the table, on the street, in the salon, etc., these decors
merely serve to better illustrate or stage certain required physical attitudes.
Precepts are duplicated and overlap in different circumstances. On a first
reading, posture seems to vary according to the social occasion. Retrospectively,
one realizes that each occasion presents variants of an invariant posture.
Conventional backgrounds, similar to the use of words in a civility
context,[56] are so many shifting pretexts for the necessity of a posture Code.
The dictates of *externum corporis decorum* reconstitute parts of the body as
well as vocal production as instances of ideal "social" appearance.

The "arts de plaire," whose chief exponents in the sixteenth century
are Castiglione, Della Casa and Guazzo, engage in a less schematized,
more strategic operation. The art of pleasing and of succeeding in society is
practiced among adults in conversation. Conversation, however, is a broad
term comprising a theory of social interaction which transcends or stops
short of verbal content. I will discuss the strategy of conversation in a
separate chapter. What is important for us here is that both sub-genres
axiomatize the body according to the same principles. Magendie refers to
them as two degrees of civility: "It goes without saying that there is no clear
demarcation line between these two domains . . . They have one thing in

common: they give rules of exclusively exterior conduct . . ."[57] While teaching how to appear virtuous, courtesy books teach virtue as appearance, i.e., as balance. In so doing they convey the specifics of deportment that Cicero only hinted at when he wrote " . . . status incessus, sessio accubitio, vultus oculi manuum motus teneat illud decorum" (". . . in standing or walking, in sitting or reclining, in our expression, our eyes, or the movements of our hands, let us preserve what we have called 'propriety' ").[58] The appearance of balance between two extremes conveying an ethical value in itself, civility prefigures the ethics of glory in the early seventeenth century.[59] I use the term ethical rather than moral because, just as virtue, measure or moderation are qualities of prudence or judgement in the Renaissance sociolect, so the polar opposite of measure is not evil but a form of imprudence which is characterized as vanity, passion or madness. The system is tautological because right and wrong do not mean good and bad as much as correct and incorrect. Therefore the correct Coded use of the body can demonstrate virtue: ". . . quod decet, honestum est," wrote Cicero, "et, quod honestum est, decet" ("Such is its [propriety's] essential nature, that it is inseparable from moral goodness; for what is proper is morally right, and what is morally right is proper").[60] In his *Galateo* Giovanni Della Casa is categorical concerning the equation of virtue and external form: " . . . in usando con le genti, essere costumato e piacevole e di bella maniera . . . e o virtu o cosa molto a virtu somigliante . . ." (" . . . using good manners, pleasantness and propriety with people is either virtue or something very close to it").[61] Physical balance only demonstrates virtue, however, when it elicits the recognition of praise. In order to solicit praise— honor and reputation—one must both conform to the norm and also transcend it. To these ends children's manuals are designed to train nature and the "arts de plaire" to naturalize training. The training of nature can be considered as an intertext for the *bassadanza* or the basse danse, whether it be found in the Civilties or the Courtisans, and it is to such a strategic reading of courtesy books that I will now turn my attention.

IV. The Pedagogical Intertext: precepts

"Nella regola una licenzia che, non essendo di regola, fosse ordinata nella regola, e potesse stare senza fare confusione o guastare l'ordine."

"A freedom to the rule, which, not being of the rule, would be ordered within it and could be there without creating confusion or ruining the actual order."

Giorgio Vasari, *Le Vite dei più eccelenti pittori, scritori e architetti* (1550).

Dancer from Cesare Negri's *Le Gratie d'Amore* (1602).

A. *The Pose as an Intertext for the Basse Danse*

Since Ingrid Brainard's work many enigmas regarding steps in the Italian and Burgundian repertory have been clarified. Yet the rationale of the pose (*posa* or *posata*) remains unexplained because its forms are not described in dance instruction books. Brainard leaves the pose as a dramatic element to be dictated *a posteriori* by the reconstructor based on what is suggested by the dance as it begins to take form and shape.[1] My contention, however, is that the pose had a formal consistency and meaning and was ideologically determined. It can only be obtained, however, intertextually.

In courtesy books, the normative body is represented frontally in an erect posture. Proper erectness is a mean between rigidity and lethargy. "Resupinare corpus," writes Erasmus, "fastus indicium est: solliter erectus, decet" ("Holding the body inordinately straight is a sign of haughtiness: let it be straight simply").[2] For Guazzo "s'ha a comporre tutto il corpo in maniera, che non paia nè tutto d'un pezzo intiero, nè tutto snodato" ("the body should be held in a way such that it is neither all of a piece nor all loose").[3] The mean is also expressed as a state of balance: "Corpus igitur aequo libramine sit erectus" ("The body should be held straight in a stable equilibrium").[4] The face is the privileged locus and the epitome of posture. Faret describes countenance as "une juste situation de tout le corps, de laquelle se forme ceste bonne mine que les femmes louent tant aux hommes: Mais elle reçoit toute sa perfection des mouvements du visage . . . Et certes on peut dire que c'est le visage qui domine au maintien extérieur . . ." ("an even stance of the whole body from which derives that expression that women praise so much in men: But all of its perfection comes from facial movements . . . And indeed one can say that the face dominates external appearance . . .").[5] Of all facial features, the eyes receive the utmost attention. "Ut ergo bene compositus pueri animus undique reluceat, relucet autem potissimum in vultu, sint oculi placidi, verecundi, compositi . . ." ("So that the good nature of a child may shine forth everywhere, and it is revealed especially on the face, let his eyes be still, modest and calm . . .").[6] Similarly, deviation from the ocular Code contaminates the appearance of the whole. "Incompositi gestus non raro viciant, non solum oculorum, verum etiam totius corporis habitum ac formam" ("Any ill-considered movements blemish not only the eyes but also the bearing and beauty of the whole body").[7]

The correct form of the glance is arrived at in two ways. It is suggested by reference to Tradition. "Picturae quidem veteres nobis loquuntur, olim singularis cuiusdam modestiae fuisse, semiclusis oculis obtueri quem admodum apud Hispanos quosdam semipetos intueri blandum haberi videtur et amicum" ("Antique pictures show us that in the old times men were of a singularly demure countenance and looked with the eyes half closed as in Spain where to look with slightly lowered eyelids is taken to be flattering and friendly").[8] The modest gaze is not turned inward. It is directed at the interlocutor. "Oculi spectent eum cui loqueris, sed placidi simplicesque, nihil procas improbumue prae se ferentes" ("Let the eyes look at him you are speaking to calmly and simply showing nothing bold or impudent").[9] Modesty has its own degrees of intensity directly proportionate to the gloriousness of the whole body. " . . . Mirentur alii tu te bene cultum esse nescias. Quò maior est fortuna, hoc est amabilior modestia" ("Let others admire you but be unaware that you are well dressed. Where fortune is greater modesty is more loved").[10] The modesty of the look fulfills a dissimulated deictic function. In being attentive, it is sufficiently uncompelling to allow the other's gaze a certain liberty. In this sense, the look is an ostensibly passive gaze which stages the body to be viewed. It corresponds to the feminine glance in the basse danse as Arbeau describes it. "Et les damoiselles avec une contenance humble, les yeulx baissez, regardans quelquefois les assistans avec une pudeur virginale" ("And the damsels with demure mien, their eyes lowered save to cast an occasional glance of virginal modesty at the onlookers").[11] The look is also, however, a glance sufficiently focused to constitute the vanishing point, as it were, of the perspective within which the interlocutor's attention is captured or engaged, prolonging the contact. In this sense, the look is an active glance staged by the body. It corresponds to the male's glance in the basse danse, "la vheue asseurée" ("a self-assured look"). In other terms, the dance analyzes the double function of the glance into distinct sexual roles.

The correct glance is also arrived at by an enumeration of every possible predication of what it should *not* be: oculi . . . non torui quod est truculentiae non improbi, quod est imprudentiae: non vagi ac volubiles, quod est insaniae . . ." ("let the eyes not be grim which is a sign of ferocity, not wanton which is a token of imprudence, not wandering and rolling which is a sign of madness . . .").[12] In this perspective, "mediocritas" is nothing but the suspension or neutralization of perverse or erroneous attitudes. All precepts follow the same procedure of elimination. Calviac writes, "la tête ne doit estre ni trop baissé [a sign of laziness], ny trop haut [a sign of arrogance]" ("the head should neither be too low [a sign of laziness], nor too high [a sign of arrogance]").[13] The correct carriage of the head mirrors that of the eyes and of the body in general. "Mais se doyt tenir droict et sans effort, car cela ha bonne grace" ("But he should hold himself straight and without effort, for that is what has grace").[14] Avoidance of lateral movements of the head also lends precision to the correct bearing. "Et ne faut point aussi que sa teste pande d'un costé ny d'autre dessus son corps, à la mode des hypocrites . . ." ("And his head shouldn't hang to one or another side of his body either, the way a hypocrite's would . . .").[15] Each facial feature is both metaphor and metonym of the same postural mean. As for the eyebrows: "sint exporrecta supercilia, non adducta, quod est tortuitatis: non sublata in altu, quod est arrogantia: non in oculos depressa, quod est male cogitantium" ("let the brows be set up and not bent which is a token of cruelty: not set up too high which is a sign of arrogance and pride nor hanging down on the eyes which is a sign of evil designs").[16] As for the cheeks: "inflare buccas fastus indicium est, easdem demittere, est animum despondentis . . ." ("to puff up the cheeks is a token of pride, to let them hang is a sign of despair . . .")[17] As for the lips: "os nec prematur quod est metuentis alterius halitu haurire, nec hiet, quod est morionum, sed leniter osculantibus se mutuo labris coniunctum sit" ("let your mouth not be sealed which is a sign that you fear the breath of another, nor let it gape which is a sign of idiocy but let the closed lips touch together softly").[18] The same principle of moderation between two extremes applies equally to the rest of the body. For example, "humeros oportet aequo libramine temperare, non in morem antennarum, alterum attolere, alterum deprimere" ("the shoulders should be evenly balanced; one shouldn't be lifted while the other is lowered").[19] One can also read that the feet should be kept practically together while standing yet slightly apart.

Just as the eyes are exemplars of correct posture, the hands are an anti-model embodying all the mistakes to which other body parts are prone. Physiognomy treatises also fulminate against hand movement. "Celuy qui s'esmeut de legier, et en parlant joüe des mains, est mauvais fol, et deceveur. Et celuy qui parle sans mouvoir ses mains est de grand entendement, est sage et preud'homme" ("He who moves about and uses his hands in speaking is deceptive and has a bad character. And he who speaks without moving his hands is wise and prudent").[20] The gestures which civility prohibits are fast, unexpected, brief, repetitve and suggestive or mimetic. Erasmus will also refer to them as gesticulation or agitation. While there are no explicit desiderata for the quality of permitted gestures, we may deduce that they are by opposition slow, smooth and separated by pauses and halts.

Similarly, the elimination of gesture in Tuccaro's second class of leaping constitutes this class as an ideal dance, an "essence." Cosme asks, " . . . pourquoy en la seconde espece de la division gymnastique avez vous faict le saut, le bal et la dance, dont on use en Europe, *sans mine, actes, ny gestes* . . ?" (" . . . why did you make the leap, ball and dance as it is used in Europe in your second class of gymnastics, *without expression, acts or gestures* . . ?").[21] The dance without gesticulation corresponds to the purity of the Greek dance for Ferrand, verifying the essence of the dance as "L'honneste exercice . . .que j'ay compris par la seconde espece . . ." ("The honorable exercise . . . that I intended as the second kind . . .").[22] Ferrand cites Atheneus as proof " . . . que la pratique et l'usage des pieds a esté premier que celuy des mains" (" . . . the practice and the use of feet came before that of hands").[23] Gestures of the hands are undesirable as they may be used to represent "quelque vicieux désir, ou deshonneste conception . . . comme sont la plus grande partie de ceux qui sont compris en la troisieme espece [mimetic dance] . . ." ("some desire suffused with vice, or some unworthy conception . . . as are most of those included in the third type [mimetic dance] . . .").[24] Gesture has no place in the essence of the dance as "bienséance": ". . . le bal et la danse qu'on faict sans gestes et mines, est une certaine espece separee des autres . . ." (". . . the ball and the dance done without gesture or expression is a certain kind distinct from the others . . .").[25]

It remains to demonstrate the pertinence of civility's Code of the pose for the basse dance. Arbeau compresses the precepts of phycial measure into two phrases applying to all dances: "Ayez la teste et le corps droit, la vheue asseurée . . ." ("Keep your head and body erect and appear self-possessed").[26] The head is mentioned first, confirming its independence from the body as transcendent element of the series. The role of the face and eyes as model is iterated by a semanticization of the glance ("asseurée"-"self-possessed") which differentiates "droit" ("erect") from Capriol's description of himself before he danced as "quasi une buche de bois" ("practically a piece of wood").[27] The precepts of physical rectitude, while calling for an immobile stance, preclude rigidity. ". . . Vos mains soient pendants, non commes mortes, ny aussi pleines de gesticulations . . ." (". . . Your hands at your sides, neither hanging limp as if dead, nor moving nervously . . .").[28] Posture approximates adherence to an imaginary center constantly remeasured between inflation and deflation. The role of the negative proposition (neither, nor) is to represent posture as a transitional moment between inaction and action where stillness is not yet motion but no longer stillness.

After the reverence, Arbeau's basse danse consists of walking hand in hand with the partner (*simples* and *doubles*) with nine halts for movements in place (*branle* and *reprise*). "Les marches et mouvements . . . de la basse danse sont pesants et graves" ("The steps and movements of the . . . basse dance are slow and solemn")[29] They should be performed " . . . marchants honnestement avec une gravité posée" (". . . walking with decorum and measured gravity").[30] For the simple the dancer steps forward on the left and steps together with the right foot. In the double he takes three consecutive steps forward (left, right and left) before stepping together with the right. There is nothing in the description which would distinguish the simple or double from walking in everyday life, such as courtesy books conceive it. Indeed, Arbeau warns that the steps should not be so big as to deform the erect posture of the upper body. ". . . Et se fault donner garde de faire les annonces des pieds si grandes qu'il semble qu'on veuille mesurer la longueur de la salle . . ." ("And you must be careful not to take strides that suggest you wish to measure the length of the hall . . .").[31] The steps of the basse dance exhibit the dancer's probity to all present by circulating two or three times through a room. The step together reminds the onlooker that the walking body is a moving posture.

A difference must be acknowledged here between the French and Italian styles. Inasmuch as "maniera" is used in the *bassadanza* there is a distinction between civil and danced walking. However, Caroso says that the "sempio" is "dalla propria natura insegnato" ("taught to oneself by one's own nature").[32] The whole relationship of dance pedagogy to social identity comes once again to the fore. We may learn to walk by learning to dance but we don't walk by dancing. Something of dance remains in the manner of the correct walk which is not dance but which would be unthinkable without dance.

The basse danse is not complete if it is not followed by the faster and lighter "tordion" or "tourdion." The "tourdion" is a slightly less energetic version of the other major Renaissance dance, the gaillard. ". . . Le tourdion n'est autre chose qu'une gaillarde par terre" (". . . The tordion is nothing other than a gaillard danced with the feet kept close to the ground").[33] Since the movements of the "tourdion" are nevertheless hopping and jumping I will approach it with a view towards its intertextual connections with civility's gestural Code.

B.   *The gestural Code as intertext for the gaillard*

My contention is that the movements of the "tourdion" complete the basse dance in that they exemplify the model body as product or, in other terms, they naturalize the Code of the pose. A brief description of the choreography is in order.

The "tourdion" or gaillard consists of what are called "les cinq pas" ("the five steps"): three hops, a jump and a pose. The hops come in a variety of forms ("greve," "ru de vache," "ruade," "entretaille," "pied croisé," "marque pied," "marque talon") because while one leg hops the other can swing front, back or sideways or else tap the floor or actually switch places with the hopping leg. Since these steps may be done either on the right leg or the left, the variety of combinations is enormous. The jump ("sault majeur") may be complicated with leg beats in which case it is called a "capriole." the landing of the jump is held as a pose ("position" or "posture"). The jump and the pose together are considered a unit called "clausulam" or "cadance." The five steps are repeated *ad infinitum* but the first three and, to a lesser degree, the fourth may be varied at each repetition. The dance therefore requires considerable mental preparation and concentration if one is to introduce variations.

If the first part of the basse danse in Arbeau's description is a paradigm of probity recalling Tuccaro's ideal second category of leaping, the gaillard recalls the fourth class, the unrefined popular dance of the day. "Ceulx qui dancent la gaillarde aujourd'huy par les villes, ilz dancent tumultuairement, et se contentent de faire les cinq pas et quelques passages sans aulcune disposition et ne se soucient pourveu qu'ilz tumbent en cadance . . ." ("In the towns nowadays the galliard is danced regardless of rules, and the dancers are satisfied to perform the five steps and a few passages without any orderly arrangement so long as they keep the rhythm . . .").[34] Once again Arbeau is reviving, if not a forgotten dance, a forgotten manner of dancing. ". . . Du commencement on la dançoit avec plus grande discretion" ("In earlier days it was danced with much more discernment").[35] Indeed, dances characterized by hopping and jumping were singled out by Renaissance polemicists for special blame. A reformist moral theology in the sixteenth century whose most articulate spokesman against dance was Lambert Daneau, equated agitated movement with madness. Roger Cosme in Tuccaro's *Trois Dialogues* attacks the dance as a mad agitation: ". . . Qui est celuy qui sans passion considerant l'agitation des personnes qui dancent avecq une telle et si grande diversité de mouvements, ne s'esmerveille de la folie de tels hommes et femmes qui s'y delectent, et ne les fuye comme personnes folles et du toute insensees?" ("Who, considering dispassionately people who dance with such diversity of movement is not astonished at the madness of such men and women who take their pleasure in it and does not flee them as people completely mad and taken leave of their senses?").[36] Daneau's critique of dancing is elaborated from certain qualities necessary to a Christian. The first quality is prudence, as his first chapter title indicates: "En matiere de recreation qu'il faut user de prudence, aussi bien qu'ailleurs, et faire choix de ce qui est licite" ("Regarding recreation one must use prudence as much as in anything else and choose what is lawful").[37] Prudence is a faculty of judgment which allows us to gauge and regulate the "honnêteté" of our own actions. His second argument is based on the form of the dance which is ". . . non convenable à gens modestes, graves, et de sens rassis" (". . .not fitting for modest, serious people with good sense").[38] The problem which form presents to stable judgment is that of diversity; first of all, the diversity of dances: "la forme est fort diverse. Car il y a branles, et encor de mille sortes, des bals, gaillardes, pavannes, corantes, voltes, et infinies autres façons" ("their form is ever changing. For there are branles, and a thousand kind of them, balls, gaillards, pavans, corantos, voltas and an infinite number of other ways").[39] The problem of diversity is also one of steps and as such is peculiar to the gaillard: "car pour tout c'est un art de sçavoir faire des cinq pas, et les diversifier . . ." ("for in sum it is the art of knowing the five steps and being able to vary them . . .").[40] Within each step bodily movement is diversified as well and, as it were, at odds with itself:

> . . . il faut bien qu'il y ait quelque autre espece de folie, c'est à dire, defaut de sons et de prudence, qui les fait sauteler et se tourmenter.

> . . . there must be some other kind of madness, that is, a defect in sense and prudence, that makes them hop about and writhe.[41]

Jumping combined the agitation of constant movement which indicated madness with the physical inflation of vanity or vainglory. By jumping the body would seem to increase its height and volume. I will refer to Montaigne in this connection, not as a specialist on the dance but as a witness to the sociolect of his time.

Montaigne's critique of bad eloquence in "des livres" centers on the "emprunt," a form of plagiarism illustrated with physical and dancing metaphors. "Ce qui les faict ainsi se charger de matiere, c'est la deffiance qu'ils ont de se pouvoir soustenir de leurs propres graces; il faut qu'ils trouvent un corps où s'appuyer . . ." ("What makes them so load themselves with material is the distrust they have of being able to sustain themselves by their own graces; they have to find a body to lean on . . .").[42] Montaigne also refers to borrowing as an "addition" to the body proper: ". . . il leur faut plus de corps. Ils montent à cheval parce qu'ils ne sont assez fort sur leurs jambes" (". . . the less wit they have, the more body they need. They mount on horseback because they are not strong enough on their legs").[43] The metaphor of dance illustrates borrowing as a "plus de corps" ("more body"), indeed a "trop de corps" ("excessive body").

> Tout ainsi qu'en nos bals, ces hommes de vile condition, qui en tiennent escole, pour ne pouvoir representer le port et la decence de nostre noblesse, cherchent à se reccomander par des sauts perilleux et autres mouvemens estranges et bateleresques. Et les Dames ont meilleur marché de leur contenance aux danses où il y a diverses descoupeures et agitation de corps, qu'en certains autres danses de parade, où elles n'ont simplement qu'à marcher un pas naturel et representer un port naïf et leur grace ordinaire.

> Just as at our balls these men of low conditon who keep dancing schools, not being able to imitate the bearing and fitness of our nobility, seek to recommend themselves by perilous leaps and other strange

mountebank antics. And the ladies can more cheaply show off their carriage in the dances where there are various contortions and twistings of the body, than in certain other formal dances where they need only walk with a natural step and display a natural bearing and their ordinary grace.[44]

By the same token, Montaigne detailed his personal non-observance of civility's precepts as a compulsive agitation of eyes, hands and feet:

> Aux lieux de ceremonie, où chacun est si bandé en contenance, où j'ay veu les dames tenir leurs yeux mesme si certains, je ne suis jamais venu à bout que quelque piece des miennes n'extravague tousjours; encore que j'y sois assis, j'y suis peu rassis. [The 1599 edition adds: 'et pour la gesticulation, ne me trouve guiere sans baguette à la main, soit à cheval ou à peid. Il y a de l'*indécence.*'] . . . On a peu dire aussi dés mon enfance que j'avois de la follie aux pieds, ou de l'argent vif, tant j'y ay de remuement et d'inconstance en quelque lieu que je les place.

> In solemn places, where everyone has such a strained expression, where I have seen the ladies keep even their eyes so steady, I have never succeeded in keeping some part of me from always wandering; even though I may be seated there, I am hardly settled there . . . So people might have said of me from my childhood that I was crazy in the feet, or had quicksilver in them, so fidgety and restless are they, wherever I place them.[45]

How is it possible then that the "tourdion" or gaillard could be part of the basse danse? I will seek the answer in civility's gestural Code.

Although civility places strict limitations on physical movement, it does contain a gestural Code. The gestural Code is intimately related to dissimulation and to nature as well as to the aesthetic enigma of grace. Permissible gesture is understood as an addition to "la disposition naturelle," and yet also as artifice or an embellishment, as Tuccaro wrote, which increases pleasure.

> . . . Le bal et la dance, dont nous avons accoustumé d'user sans faire aucuns gestes, se pratiquoit ainsi des anciens long temps avant tout autre exercice, bien que depuis, l'invention des hommes *aye adjousté à la disposition naturelle* quelques artifices et embellissements pour donner davantage de plaisir . . .

> . . . The ball and the dance as we are accustomed to it, without any gesture, was practiced by the Ancients a long time before any other exercises, although since then men's inventions *have added some artifice and embellishments to natural disposition* to give more pleasure . . .[46]

Erasmus states the theory of gesture near the beginning of *De Civilitate Morum Puerilium:* "... contra [gestus] compositi, quod natura decorum est reddunt decentius: quod vitiosum est, si non tollunt, certé tegunt minuuntque" ("... ordered and natural gestures give grace: if they don't eliminate faults at all events they attenuate and mask them").[47] One can find gestures in Erasmus which exercise a corrective or masking function, the most frequent one being that of turning away: "Si aliis presentibus incidat sternutatio, civile est corpus avertere" ("If he sneezes in someone's presence, it is proper to turn aside").[48] Turning away is complemented by a series of subsequent attenuating gestures.

> ... Mox ubi se remiserit impetus, fignareos crucis imagine, de in sublato pileo resalutatis que vel salutarant vel salutare debuerant ... pueri est aperire caput.

> ... Once the attack has subsided, he should make the sign of the cross and take off his hat to those who are about to bless him or should be ... a child should remove his cap.[49]

Yawning is another facial deformation which gesture may make amends for. "Si fors urgeat oscitatio, nec datur averti, aut cedere, strophio volane tegatur os, mox imagine crucis obsignetur" ("If you cannot avoid opening your mouth and there is no way to turn aside or withdraw, cover your mouth with a handkerchief or the palm of your hand and make the sign of the cross").[50] Laughter is another involuntary act which threatens to deform the poise of the face and, indeed, of the whole body. Erasmus flatly prohibits the latter eventuality. "Cachinnus et immodicus ille totum corpus quatiens risus, quem ob id Graeci concussorem appellant, nulli decoris est atati, nedum pueritiae" ("Loud and unbridled laughter which shakes the whole body which the Greeks called *risus syncrusius,* the shaker, is not becoming to any age and certainly not to a child").[51] Here again, a deviation from prescribed posture is a sign of vice. "Sic autem vultus hilaritatem exprimat, ut necoris habitum dehonestet, nec animum dissolutum arguat" ("The face can express hilarity without anything dishonorable or betraying a dissolute nature").[52] Vice is identified with error and virtue with knowledge. There are nevertheless corrective gestures for the laugh that might overpower composure. "Et si qua res adeo riducula inciderit, ut volentibus eiusmodi risum exprimat, mappa manuué tegenda facies" ("And if something so laughable occurs that one cannot hold back laughter, do it covering your face with a napkin or your hand").[53] An equivalent series of coded gestures applies to nasal excretions:

> A naribus absit mucoris purulentia, quod est sordidorum ... strophiolis excipere narium recrementa decorum, idque *paulisper averso corpore,*

si qui adsint honoratiores. Si quid in solum deiectum est, emuncto
duobus digitis nasa, mox *pede proterendum* est.

Mucous in the nose is something filthy people have ... it is decent to use
a handkerchief, *turning aside* for a little while if someone commanding
respect is present. If it falls on the floor, one should clean the nose *with
two fingers* and *trample on it.*[54]

Similar instructions can, on occasion, find their way into Arbeau's rules for
dancing as well. ". . . Crachez et mouchez peu, et si la nécessité vous y
constrainct, tornés le visage d'aultre part et usez d'un beau mouchoir blanc..."
("Spit and blow your nose sparingly, or if needs must turn your head away
and use a fair white handkerchief").[55]

There is, however, a second aspect to the gestural Code. "Ordered
and natural gestures give grace . . ." Quintilian makes an equally cryptic
comment in his discussion of oratorical action. "Gesture and movement are
also productive of grace..."[56] We have progressed from grace as an overall
effect of corporal propriety to grace as a specific attribute of movement.
"Du côté du sujet," writes the twentieth-century aesthetician Raymond
Bayer, "la grâce est esthétique de *l'aisance* ... Elle est faite d'une technique
de la sûreté intérieure."[57] Apart from the often cited mistakes, the only
major error or vice that requires concealment is the visibility of the
behavioral Code as Code. The role of grace is to conceal coded behavior
with a natural appearance. Gesture affords the diversity without which the
Code of civility would become predictable, visible and thereby discredited.
Montaigne describes two forms of "contenances desreglées" as regards
civil conduct. Both are errors of predictability:

Je desirasse d'aucuns Princes que je connois, qu'ils en fussent [des
révérences] plus espargnans, et justes dispensateurs; car, ainsin
indiscrettement espanduës, elles ne portent plus de coup. Si elles sont
sans esgard, elles sont sans effet. Entre les contenances desreglées,
n'oublions pas la morgue de Constantius l'Empereur, qui en publicq
tenoit tousjours la teste droite, sans la contourner ou flechir ny ca ny là,
non pas seulement pour regarder ceux qui le saluoient à costé, ayant le
corps planté immobile, sans se laisser aller au branle de son coche, sans
oser ny cracher, ny se moucher, ny essuyer le visage devant ses gens.

I could wish that certain princes I know would be more sparing and just
in dispensing these salutes; for when they are thus strewn about
indiscriminately, they have no more power. If they are given without
consideration, they are given without effect. Among the extraordinary
mannerisms, let us not forget the arrogance of the Emperor Constantius,

> who in public always held his head straight, without turning or bending
> it this way or that, not even to look at those who saluted him from the
> side; keeping his body fixed and motionless, without letting himself
> move with the swaying of his coach, without daring either to spit, or to
> blow his nose, or to wipe his face in front of people.[58]

Lack of moderation in the application of civility's precepts can be as great a
fault as lack of measure itself. Arbeau remarks that the dance ". . .
apporteroit mespris à celluy qui comme un pillier de salle y seroit trop
assidu" (". . . dance would bring contempt upon one who became over
zealous . . .").[59] Gesture or movement is the prism through which all other
precepts can be bent. The rules of its use defy codification.

> Elles [les civilités] ont quelques formes penibles, lesquelles, pourveu
> qu'on oublie par discretion, non par erreur, on n'en a pas moins de
> grace. J'ay veu souvent des hommes incivils par trop de civilité, et
> importuns de courtoisie.

> They [the laws of our French civility] have some troublesome forms,
> which a man may forget, provided he does so by discretion and not by
> mistake, without losing grace by his behavior. I have often seen men
> uncivil by too much civility, and importunate in courtesy.[60]

Erasmus' natural gesture which produces grace, like Castiglione's
famous "sprezzatura," can only be defined negatively as that which is
unaffected. It is a "je-ne-sais-quoi" which could be likened to the
emergence of a "merveilleux" from within the Renaissance's moral
technology of the act. One must "usar in ogni cosa una certa sprezzatura,
che nasconda l'arte, e dimostri cio, che fisa, e dice, venir fatto senza fatica, e
quasi sensa pensarvi. Da questo credo io che derivi assai la gratia . . ."
("practice in all things a certain *sprezzatura* [nonchalance], so as to conceal
all art and make whatever is done or said appear to be without effort and
almost without any thought about it. And I believe much grace comes of
this . . .").[61] Though naturalness is a carefully contrived appearance of non-
assiduity, the natural gesture cannot be coded as uncoded without defeating
its own purpose. "Non v'accorgete, che questo, che voi in M. Roberto
chiamate sprezzatura è vera affettatione? perche chiaramente si conosce,
che esto si sforza con ogni studio mostrar di non pensarvi e questo è il
pensarvi troppo" (". . . What you are calling nonchalance . . . is really
affectation, because we clearly see him making every effort to show that he
takes no thought of what he is about, which means taking too much
thought . . .").[62] Precepts may stipulate a given posture, but the end product
escapes definition. "Toutes les bonnes parties que nous avons alleguées, sont
tres-considerables en un Gentilhomme, mais le comble de ces choses consiste

en une certaine grace naturelle, qui en tous ses exercices, et jusques à ses moindres actions doit reluire comme un petit rayon de Divinité . . ." ("All the parts that we have noted are very important for a gentleman, but the height of these things consists in a certain natural grace which shines through all his exercises and appears even in his least actions like a divine spark . . .).[63] Instruction is ultimately a matter of imitation. "Tout le conseil qui se peut donner en cela, c'est que ceux qui ont un bon jugement pour reigle de leur conduite, s'ils ne se sentent douez de ce sublime don de nature, taschent du moins à reparer ce manquement par l'imitation des plus parfaits exemples, et de ceux qui auront l'approbation generale" ("The only advice that can be given in this is that those who have good judgment, if they do not feel themselves sublimely gifted by nature, should try to overcome this lack by imitating the most perfect examples and those who have general approbation").[66] Courtesy books initiate an unending process of mastery of the body through imitation; the courtier imitates him who is most successful at transcending collective control and who therefore extends the boundaries of the permissible by appearing natural. Just as each bodily feature perfects its bearing by modeling itself on the composure of the body as a whole, the general composure is made up of the harmony of individual features. The same procedure holds true for the "social body." Conformity results in a confusion between biology and the law in that regulation and spontaneity seem to presuppose one another. Failing genius, one conforms to the divine aptitude in others. So, writes Guazzo, "si veste della cognitione di se stesso per mezo della civil conversatione . . ." ("one arrives at knowledge of oneself through the means of civil conversation . . .").[65] Civility functions as an institution, a self-perpetuating ideology in practice, in that each deviation from the Code which falls short of brilliant transgression is noticed by others and discreetly brought to the attention of the uninstructed. "Finalmente ci contentiamo," writes Guazzo, "di sottoporci alle communi opinioni, e ci veniamo a ravvedere di qualche nostra imperfettione, la quale ci sforziamo di correggere secondo il giudicio altrui" ("We are happy to submit ourselves to the common opinion and we manage to mend some imperfection which we try to correct thanks to others' judgment").[66] Because movement is said to reflect simultaneously a perfect conformity to a norm of propriety and the flowering of an innate quality (prudence as individual nature or "complexion"), it is unrepresentable. Therefore, the specificity of the dancing body in dance treatises is also passed over in silence.

But movement is not unrepresentable solely because its role is to naturalize the pose. It is not sufficient in the system of civility that physical discipline be made to appear spontaneous according to what Bayer calls "l'esthétique de la résorption des contrôles."[67] "Le domaine," writes

Bayer, "de la spontanéité soudain s'élargit, et la *sprezzatura* y fait entrer tous les contrôles. C'est la vigilance, à son tour, qui devient spontanée . . . le contrôle, transfiguré, vient jouer de verve avec la verve."[68] I do not agree that the control Code of the pose is literally transfigured any more than I agree with the opposite extreme as Pierre Legendre expressed it: "le contraire de l'orthodoxie est la folie."[69] A form of permitted idiosyncracy, originality or gesture emerging from the systemic does exist, corresponding roughly to what Stephen Greenblatt has called "individual self fashioning."[70] Grace witnesses to the clandestine reintroduction of madness into the system. Grace dissimulates artifice behind a second nature: movement. Arbeau tells us that the gaillard must be danced by someone who already possesses the qualities necessary for its performance. "La gaillarde est appellée ainsi parce qu'il fault estre gaillard et dispos pour la danser . . ." ("The galliard is so called because one must be gay and nimble ['gaillard'] to dance it . . .").[71] Similarly, when Capriol first hears of the jump one must perform in the gaillard, the "capriole," he underlines his own natural predisposition to the step in an onomastic code. "J'apprendray volontiers ceste capriole puis qu'elle porte mon nom . . ." ("I shall willingly learn this *capriole* as it bears my name").[72] The dancing body is absent from dance treatises because movement, being by definition a product of the genius or inspiration of a unique personal nature, cannot be analysed. It is not sufficient to speak of a natural gesture versus an acquired one in order to elucidate the system. An example from Pierre Charron serves to illustrate this point. Charron posed the possibility of a hyperbolically natural gesture which might transcend the distinction of the natural versus the acquired gesture.

> Comm'il y en à, qui ont des contenances, gestes, et mouvements artificiels et affectés, aussi y en a, qui en ont de si naturels et si propres, qu'ils ne les sentent, ny ne les recognoissent point, comme pencher la teste, rincer le nais, Mais tous en avons, qui ne partent point de nostre discours, ains d'une pure naturelle et prompte impulsion, comme mettre la main au devant en nos cheutes.

> Just as some have expressions, gestures and movements which are artifical and affected, so there are others whose movements are so natural and indigenous to them that they don't sense them or recognize them, such as leaning one's head to one side or tugging at one's nose. But we all have some which don't derive from our reason but from a pure, natural and prompt impulse as when we extend an arm to break a fall.[73]

The three types of gesture correspond to three degrees of propriety:

Distinction de la vraie prudhommie, en vertu naturelle et en vertu acquise: *il y a encore une troisième composée des deux; ce qui constitue trois degrés* de perfection. *Pour achever cette perfection, il faut la grâce de Dieu . . .*

Distinction of true uprightness into natural and acquired virtue: *there is a third kind composed of these two, which constitutes three degrees* of perfection. *To arrive at this perfection one needs God's grace . . .*[74]

Movement naturalizes the pose but the combination of the two together, their compound so to speak, absolves the pose of the need to furnish further proofs. Castiglione uses the example of the dance to explain the persuasive power of hyperbolically natural movement.

Qual di voi e che non rida, quando il nostro M. Pierpaulo danza alla foggia sua, con que saltetti, e gambe stirate in punta di piede, senza mover la testa, come se tutto fosse un legno con tanta attentione, che di certo pare che vada numerando i passi? Qual occhio è cosi cieco, che non vegga in questola disgratia dell'affettatione, et la gratia in molti huomini, et done, che sono qui presenti, di quella sprezzata desinvoltura (che ne i movimenti del corpo cosi la chiamano) con un parlar, ò ridere, ò adattarsi, mostrando non estimar, e pensar più ad ogni altra cosa che à quello, per far creder a chi vede quasi di non saper, ne poter errare.

Who among you fails to laugh when our messer Pierpaolo dances after his own fashion, with those capers of his, his legs stiff on tiptoe, never moving his head, as if he were a stick of wood, and all this so studied that he really seems to be counting his steps? What eye is so blind as not to see in this the ungainliness of affectation; and not to see the grace of that cool *disinvoltura* [ease] (for when it is a matter of bodily movements many call it that) in many of the men and women here present, who seem in words, in laughter, in posture not to care; or seem to be thinking more of everything than of that, so as to cause all who are watching them to believe that they are almost incapable of making a mistake?[75]

The effect of movement on the spectator is also to prevent him from analyzing and consequently criticizing mistakes. The term "gaillard" brings me back to the rhetorical intertext. The dancer ". . . can, by his movements, without uttering a single word, make himself understood and persuade spectators that he is spirited [gaillard] and worthy of being praised, loved and cherished." Movement can perfect the pose just as emotion overtakes and completes the task of charm, just as the orator's established moral character relieves him from considering the audience's disposition.

In order to accomplish this, however, movement must infiltrate the pose. There are elements of movement within the pose in the basse danse and of the pose within movement in the gaillard. Together they can be elucidated with the help of a notion developed by the fifteenth-century Italian dance theorists: *fantasmata*.

C.   *Measure as a practical dancing term: "fantasmata"*

There are two movements in Arbeau's description of the basse danse which, while stationary, distort the postural Code of the pose. By distorting the postural Code of the pose I mean disturbing the straight vertical line of erect posture and not necessarily the decomposition of movement into several impulses or simultaneous parts. These two movements are the *branle* and the *reprise*. The first is a "pliement de corps" ("bending the body") and the other is a "iactation(s) de piedz" ("twitching the feet"). Arbeau's description of the *branle* is as follows:

> . . . en tenant les pieds joincts, remuant le corps doucement du cousté gauche pour la premiere mesure, puis du cousté droit, en regardant les assistants modestement pour la deuxieme mesure, puis encore du cousté gauche pour la troisieme mesure: Et pour la quatrieme mesure du cousté droit, en regardant la Damoiselle d'une oeillade desrobée doulcement et discretement.

> . . . by keeping the heels together and moving the body gently to the left for the first bar; then to the right, glancing modestly the while at the spectators, for the second bar, then again to the left for the third. And for the fourth bar, to the right again with a discreetly tender sidelong glance at the damsel.[76]

While the *branle* step should not be confused with the dance type of the same name, Burgundian sources show the feet moving from side to side. With this in mind Brainard has described the step as "a swaying motion from side to side."[77] Arbeau's description suggests a twisting of the upper body from side to side (*branler* in French simply means to move and the verb *remuer* in the above cited description means the same) which would liken it to the Italian *campeggiare* which will be explained shortly. The "branle" may also have ressembled an abbreviated reverence called *congé* by Arbeau: ". . . A voir le geste du danseur, il sembleroit qu'il voulust finir et prendre congé, et neantmoins après le branle, il continue ses marches et mouvements . . ." (". . . from the gesture of the dancer it appears as if he were about to finish and take leave of the damsel, although in fact he proceeds with the steps and movements as set down . . .").[78]

The Burgundian *reprise* (also called *desmarche*) also differs from the description Arbeau gives. Brainard interprets as follows: ". . . draw the right foot behind the left, raise and lower the body while doing so."[79] She also notes that because of its lifting and falling motion the *reprise* recalls the Italian stylistic term *ondeggiare*. The terms *campeggiare* and *ondeggiare* are technical components of *fantasmata:* the profile of common stylistic preoccupation can be intimated from these relationships. For Arbeau, the *reprise* consists of shaking both legs: ". . . lequel vous ferez en remuant un peu les genoux, ou les pieds, ou les artoils seullement, comme si les pieds vous fremioient . . ." ("You will perform it by moving the knees gently from side to side, or the feet, or the toes only, as if your feet were trembling").[80] It is not specified whether the foot or leg is touching the floor or lifted in the air as it vibrates. Linguistically speaking, "reprise" can mean refrain, i.e., the repetition of the shaking movement. To sum up, despite certain differences in interpretation, in both the *branle* and the *reprise* the body is no longer vertical but begins to bend, either from above or below.

Quintilian concedes that movement may infiltrate the pose at the expense of what is seemly but in the interests of what is expedient. Similarly, in courtesy books, movement naturalizes the overly disciplined aspect of training implicit in the pose.

> The body when held bolt upright has but little grace, for the face looks straight forward, the arms hang by the sides, the feet are joined and the whole figure is stiff from top to toe. But that curve, *I might almost call it motion,* with which we are so familiar, gives an impression of action and animation.[81]

The pose, however, can also infiltrate movement. For example, the gaillard consists almost exclusively of hops and leaps although its choreography never once calls for a distortion of the upright posture as do the *branle* or the *reprise.* Furthermore, as has already been pointed out, each recurring sequence of the gaillard is concluded by a motionless pose called "posture." While the scandal of the basse danse is movement within the pose, the scandal of the gaillard is the pose within movement. Thus while the basse danse alternates movement and the pose as distinct units of two choregraphic sequences (the basse danse and the "tourdion"), it also comprises a series of microalternations of movement and pose within the dancing body. Fifteenth-century Italian treatises, and particularly the work of Domenico da Piacenza, create an analogous tension between movement and the pose which can be studied through the *doppio*. I will approach it by moving from the concept of measure to that of "fantasmata" and then show the way Arbeau extrapolates the same conceptual system.

In the fifteenth-century Italian dance treatises, "misura" (measure) is one of the five or six "particelle principali" of the dance. Guglielmo Ebreo describes measure as follows in "Capitulum de Misura":

Misura, in questa parte et all'arte del danzare appartenente, s'intende una dolcie e misurata concordanza di vocie e di tempo partito con ragione et arte, il quale principalmente consiste nello strumento citarizante o altro suono, el quale in tal modo sia concordante e temperato, che tanto sia il suo pieno, quanto il suo voto. Cio è che tanto sia il tinore, quanto il contratinore, tale che sia l'un tempo misuratamente, el quale a l'altro per lui (quale bisogna che la persona che vuole danzare) si regoli e misuri et a quello perfettamente si concordi ne'suoi movimenti si (e) in tal modo, che i suoi passi siano al detto tempo e misura perfettamente concordanti e colla detta misura regolati, e che intenda e conosca qual piè debba andare al pieno, e quale al voto, portando la sua persona libera colli giesti suoi alla detta misura . . .

Measure in this section as a component of the art of dance means a sweet and measured concordance of voices and tempo divided with reason and art, which measure consists above all in string instruments or other sounds which are concordant and temperate in such manner, that they are by turns full and empty. That is to say they are by turns the tenor and the countertenor so that a tempo may be called measured which besides is regulated by him (the dancer) and perfectly harmonized in his movements in such a way that his steps are perfectly concordant with the said tempo and measure. The dancer must know which foot should go to the fullness and which to the void, carrying his person freely with his gestures according to said measure.[82]

Otto Kinkeldey's understanding of measure is an oversimplification. "This clearly refers," he writes, "to the dancer's ability to keep time. It is the musical sense of rhythm and proportion, applied by the dancer to the sound of an instrument with plucked strings (*strumento citarizante*) or some other music."[83] It is true that at times measure simply means meter. But the term is far more complex. For Ingrid Brainard measure is a choreographic principle of rhythmic order (the partitioning of a melody into "choreographie-bedingte Abschnitte") thanks to which distinct compositions were realizable. This is doubtless true but it does not exhaust the meaning of the term. A metaphorical network of other terms (notably fullness and emptiness, speech and silence) points to the esthetic and technical connotations of the term for the dancing body.

As the text cited above reveals, there is a concordant relationship between the dancing body and measure. However, measure itself is a concordance in music between the "low" and the "high" notes and between "fullness" and the "void" ("il pieno" and "il voto"). The *tinore* or tenor was the *canto fermo*, plain song or unadorned melody to which the higher descant was added (the *contratinore*) creating the polyphony of basse danse music. The "low" of the *canto fermo* parallels "fullness" and the "high" of the descant parallels the "void." Furthermore, "lowness" and "fullness" parallel the pose since the basse danse, emblematic of the pose, is danced low as its name indicates. Similarly, highness and the void parallel movement since the gaillard or "tourdion," or in the Italian system the *saltarello,* are performed aloft. Domenico da Piacenza divides the motion of the dance into nine natural and three accidental movements. In so doing he designates "fullness" as speech and the "void" as silence.

> Le novi naturalli operati sono in lo pieno e li tre accidentalli operati sono in lo vuodo. E per che bene dica el filosopho che non se po dare vuodo dico vuodo el tacere e pino lol dire dico vuodo tra uno tempo el altro dico pieno in nel tempo instanti . . .

> The nine natural acts are in the fullness and the three accidental acts are in the void. And the philosopher says that there cannot be a void [*vuodo*]. I say that the void is silence and the fullness [*pino*] is speech and that the void is between one beat and the next, and that the fullness is on the instant of the beat . . .[84]

Thus, in one sense, "fullness" and the "void" are accented and unaccented beats.[85] However, this partial definition by no means exhausts the sense of measure since measure is said by Cornazano to consist in a quick descent on an unaccented beat:

> Ancora nel dançare non solamente s'observa la misura de gli soni, ma una misura la quale non è musicale, ançi fore di tutte quelle, che è un misurare l'aere nel levamento dell'ondeggiare, cioè che sempre s'alçi [si alzi] a un modo; che altrimenti si romperia misura. L'ondeggiare non e altro che uno alçamento tardo di tutta la persona et l'abbassamento presto.

> Also in dancing one must observe a measure which is not only that of sounds but a non-musical measure, apart from the others mentioned. It is a measuring of the air in the elevation of the undulation [*ondeggiare.*] One must rise in a way so as not to break measure. Undulation [*ondeggiare*] is nothing other than a gradual lifting of the whole person and a precipitous lowering.[86]

The term "ondeggiare" first appears in Cornazano coupled with the unexplained term "campeggiare," and subsequently often in the context of "maniera": "*Maniera* é, che . . . dovete dare aptitudine a le cose che facite, campeggiando et ondeggiando colla persona, secondo el pede che movite" ("The rule of Manner . . . you must perform with aplomb applying the movements of 'campeggiare' and 'ondeggiare' according to the foot that is in motion").[87] Mazzi suggests that if "ondeggiare" is a movement on a vertical plane, "campeggiare" might signify a comparable horizontal movement but doesn't specify further. Kinkeldey hypothesizes that "campeggiare" refers to the stillness of the pose: "With the significance of our English expression, 'camping out,' equivalent to 'settling down,' in mind, I prefer to translate the dance term *campeggiare* to posture, to pose or to balance, thus making a distinction between the up and down undulation and a contrasting quiet pose or balance."[88] Inglehearn and Forsyth, following in the footsteps of Kinkeldey, translate "campeggiare" to balance.[89] Brainard translates "campeggiare" as spreading out. It appears, however, if we compare Cornazano and Guglielmo Ebreo on "maniera," that the former's "campeggiando" is the latter's "ombreggiando": a lateral "shading" movement.

The name of the basic Renaissance step is the "simple" ("sciempio"): a step forward and together so that both feet are touching as they were before the step began. There are no Italian descriptions of the simple but Arbeau describes it clearly. Although this step constitutes a movement, the upper body is transported in one block and remains, as it were, motionless. "Maniera" is explained by Guglielmo Ebreo not as the vertical "ondeggiato" (undulation) but as a horizontal "ombreggiato" (shadowing) during the "simple." In "ombreggiato" the upper body turns away from the direction of the step and looks over the stationary leg.

> E questo s'intende, che quando alcuno nell'arte del danzare faciesse o vero uno passo sciempio, o vero uno passio doppio, portasse che quello, secondo accade, lo adorni et ombreggi con bella maniera, cioè che dal piè che lui porta el passo sciempio o vero passo doppio, infino che'l tempo misurato dura, tutto si volti colla sua persona in su quello lato o collo piè manco, overo col piè ritto collo quale lui abbi a fare il detto atto adornato et ombreggiato dalla detta regola, chiamata Maniera, la quale nella pratica più largamente si porrà compreendere . . .

> Manner is when in the art of dance one performs a simple or a double step, either one should be adorned and shadowed with agreeable manner. That is that from the foot that initiated the simple or double and as long as the measure lasts, the whole person turns to the side (right foot or left) on which one has to perform the said adornment or shading of the rule, called *Manner*, all of which will become clearer during practice.[90]

Although Cornazano does not manage to define "campeggiando" explicitly, the presence of the term within the description is sufficient to grasp its meaning, especially when compared to Guglielmo Ebreo's discussion of "maniera."

> ... Comme è se movite el dritto per fare uno doppio, dovete campeggiare sopra el sinistro che rimane in terra, volgendo alquanto la persona a quella parte, et ondeggiare nel sicondo passo curto lavandovi soavemente sopra quello, e con tal suavita abassarvi al terço che compisse el doppio.

> If you move the right foot to perform a double, you should pause over [*campeggiare*] the left which remains on the ground, turning one's person somewhat to that side, and rise up slightly [*ondeggiare*] in the second briefer step in a smooth lift, and lower oneself again with the same smoothness on the third which completes the double.[91]

Having established the sense of "ondeggiare" as a slow rising and a precipitous falling movement it can now be equated with measure.

> E nota che questa agilitade e mainera per niuno modo vole essere adoperata per li estremi. Ma tenir el mezo del tuo movimento che non sia ni troppo ni poco, cum tanta suavita de che paxi una gondola che da dinrimi spinta sia per quelle undicelle quando el mare fa quieta segondo sua natura. Alçando le dicte undicelle cum tardezza et asbata dosse cum presteza. Sempre operando el fondamento y de la causa cioe *mexura laquale e tardeza Ricoperada cum presteza.*

> And note that this agility and manner should by no means be adapted to extremes. One should hold the middle of one's movement which is to say one should be neither excessive nor lacking [*ni troppo ni poco*]. One should employ the smoothness with which a gondola passes, pushed along by little waves when the sea is tranquil as is her nature. These little waves lift one gradually and lower one precipitously, always following the basis and cause of *measure which is hesitation overcome by promptness.*[92]

Measure, therefore, is the theory of that motion in dance which rises slowly and drops back quickly. Curiously, measure designates both the golden mean ("tenir el mezo del tuo movimento"–"hold the middle of one's movement") and a perceptible difference of height and depth, underlined by a rhythmic contrast: it is an ethical principle and the theory of a physical technique.

The theoretical status of the principle of measure as "tardeza Ricoperada cum presteza" ("hesitation overcome by promptness") establishes the characteristic Renaissance dance movement, not choreographically but stylistically speaking, as an alternation of motion and pose in which one is constantly overtaking, indeed invading, the other, both sequentially and spatially, that is both in the same moment and in succeeding moments. Measure signifies the relationship between movement and the pose which is neither one nor the other but each in their transition to the other. This transitional moment is called "fantasmata" by Domenico.

> Oltra dico a ti chi del mestiero vole imparar bisogna danzare per fantasmata et nota che fantasmata è una presteza corporale laquale e mossa cum lo intelecto de la mexura dicta imprima disopra facendo requia acadauno tempo che pari haver veduto lo capo di meduxa como dice el poeta cioe che facta el motto su tutto di piedra inquello instante et ininstante mitti ale como falcone . . .

> And also I tell you that in this *métier* which you wish to learn there is need to dance with *fantasmata;* and note that this *fantasmata* consists of bodily rapidity motivated by an understanding of the [rhythmic] measure described above, whereby, during each bar one gives an instant's pause as though having seen the Medusa's head, as says the poet: that is to say that, having made a movement, one is in that instant as though turned to stone, and in the next instant takes wing like the falcon . . .[93]

Brainard is on the right track when she says that there is no real pause but only a pose.[94] Yet the notion of "energiegeladener Spannungspause zwischen den Bewegungen" is not dialectical enough to render Domenico's meaning. First of all, *fantasmata* is not a quality peculiar to either movement or the pose, but rather one inherent in their interplay. Furthermore, poses are an integral part of much of Domenico's choreography (intentionally transgressing his taxonomy Brainard classes them among the "motti naturali"-"natural movements"), while the phenomenon of *fantasmata* is valid for each bar ("acadauno tempo") and therefore can be applied constantly. Domenico calls *fantasmata* "una presteza corporale" ("bodily rapidity"). "Presteza" is a quality of moving toward the pose: of the quick descent into "fullness," "speech" and "lowness" ("asbata dosse cum presteza"-"precipitously lowered").

A similar conceptual system can be remarked in Arbeau's *Orchesographie*. Arbeau calls the jump ("saut majeur") preceding the "posture" in the gaillard, a silence. The jump, as the following passage indicates, would seem to rise slowly, in accordance with the Italian theories. It will be remembered that "cadance" designated the combination of the jump and the pose:

> Cadance n'est aultre chose qu'un sault majeur suivy d'une posture: Et comme vous voiez qu'ès chansons musicales, les joueurs d'instruments

ayans joué l'accord penultime, *se taisent un peu de temps:* Puis jouent le dernier accord pour faire fin doulce et harmonieuse, ainsi le sault majeur qui est quasi comme un silence des pieds, et *cessation de mouvements* est cause que la posture qui le suyt ha meilleure grace, et se treuve plus aggreable . . .

Cadence is simply a *saut majeur* followed by a posture. You have observed in a musical composition how musicians *pause for a moment* after the penultimate chord before playing the final chord in order to make an agreeable and harmonious ending: thus, the *saut majeur,* which is almost like a silence of the feet and *a pause in movement,* enhances the grace of the succeeding *posture* and creates a more pleasing effect.[95]

In this passage the pause before the descent into posture suggests, though in different terms, a slow ascent and, forcibly, a quick descent. It is particularly interesting that in the case of jumping this is practically impossible to execute. The metaphor of musical instruments which pause (presumably while the dancer is in the air, on the penultimate chord) is accompanied by something "like . . . a pause in movement." In other terms, the slow ascent is suggested here as a pause in the air. Therefore the "saut majeur" can be called both a "silence," belonging to "highness," *and* an end to movement ("cessation de mouvements") because it is already an incipient pose, about to alight. Brainard comments extensively on the correspondance of the above-cited passage of Arbeau with Domenico. She sees it as a proof of the faithful transmission of dances and steps from generation to generation (". . . ein neuerliches Beispiel für die Treue, mit welcher ganze Tänze ebenso wie einzelne Schritte oder Schrittfolgen von Generation zu Generation weitergereicht werden, ohne ihre ursprüngliche Gestalt zu verlieren").[96]

Fantasmata denotes movement as the phantom of itself, about to stop but not yet in stasis. It also designates the pose as the transition from statue to animation. It is therefore imprecise to say, as does zur Lippe, that "the pose and fantasmata conditioned one another."[97] *Fantasmata*, rather, defines dancing as a compromise between movement and the pose, a transitional act in which each seems about to become the other. The pose is animated from within and movement carries the body from one tonic pose to another. An analogy could be made with a film strip in which the movement of figures is produced by a sequence of what are in reality still photographs. Paradoxically, the moment in which the most emphatic movement occurs is the moment of its percussive cessation or freezing in the pose. In other terms, movement calls the most attention to itself as movement when its own forward impetus is precipitously broken and exchanged for an unexpected stillness. When Domenico writes that the body should be breathing through *fantasmata* ("spirando el corpo *p* fantasmata")[98] it is more likely that stillness corresponds to the end of breath than that postures should be floated "on an actual breath."[99] Cornazano posits stillness as a silence ("tacere" - "quieting down") in which the body dies and then comes back to life: "Talhor tacere un tempo e starlo morto non e brutto, ma entrare poi nel seguente con aeoroso modo quasi come persona che susciti da morte a vita" ("To quiet down for a time and be as dead is not ugly, and then in the next part to be as one resuscitated from the dead with an airy manner").[100] The other emphasis on movement occurs between the break from the pose (taking wing like the falcon) and the slow gradual ascent (of the gondola) characterizing *ondeggiare*.

The compromise between movement and pose is also phrased by Domenico as an agreement of the body to an agreement between high and low sounds, the conformity of the body to a compromise in sound. As parallels to "high" and "low," the "void" and "fullness" can easily refer to pitch. The notion of *fantasmata* itself doubtless owes much to Renaissance concepts of the harmony of contraries. This, however, is a direction for further research. In what follows I will limit myself to showing how one spoke about movement by speaking about the voice.

V.   The Political Intertext: conversation

"... Je puis dire avoir contenté en un corps bien proportionné, l'oeil, l'oreille, et l'entendement."

"... I can say I have satisfied the eye, the ear and the understanding in a well proportioned body."

Balthazar de Beaujoyeulx, *Le Balet Comique de la Royne,* 1581

Group of dancers from Cesare Negri's *Le Gratie d'Amore* (1602).

A. *The Interpretant*

In this chapter I shall elaborate a model for the interaction between dancer and spectator based on the voice in conversation. My model will be developed from a reading of Stefano Guazzo's *La Civil Conversatione*. This work consists of a series of dialogues between il Cavalier Guglielmo convalescing from a severe illness and a friend who visits him, the doctor and philosopher Annibale Magnocavalli (I will call him Annibale as does the text). The contrasts between Castiglione and Guazzo are well-known.[1] The epitome of etiquette in 1528, which Castiglione designated with the neologism *sprezzatura*, was elaborated by Guazzo in 1574 within a more pragmatic field of operation which he called "conversatione." Conversing is a broad theme in Guazzo's text delimited chiefly by its opposition to solitude in order to convey the idea of community or consortship. Although it was frequently read and translated in the Renaissance and delves further into the mechanisms of social exchange than do other courtesy books I have not chosen Guazzo's text because it is especially representative of the "art de plaire" genre. I have chosen it, rather, as a textual interpretant. The term interpretant has been proposed by Michael Riffaterre for signs or texts which ". . . contain a model of the equivalences and transferrals from one code to the other . . . ."[2] In the language of dance treatises, dance is "a" civility and "a" rhetoric in that its theory is a juncture between persuasion and urbanity. Therefore, courtesy books are an intertext for dance treatises with regard to precepts. Civility's theory of conversational interaction is the intertext for the dancing body's effect on the spectator because in Guazzo's text, conversation is rendered by a rhetorical code. The rhetorical code thus becomes the interpretant joining text to intertext: ultimately, the theory of the interaction of dance to the theory of the interaction of conversation. Without the interpretant the analysis would be caught in an ideological circle, a term which Louis Marin has used to describe the vicious because tautologous circularity of an epistemology in which model and example appear interchangeable (dance as "a kind of" rhetoric, rhetoric as "a kind of" urbanity, urbanity as "a kind of" dance, etc.). "This complementarity," writes Marin, "acts in such a way that no one notion appears alone except as angled in the light of the other one."[3]

References to oratorical action usurp the place of a clear explanation of the techniques of conversation in *La Civil Conversatione*: ". . . [mentre] si ponga un poco di studio nell'attione, ò sia nel suono delle parole, il quale, se ben considerate, ha forza di far parere quel che non è, o piu di quell che visia" (". . . we just have to give some attention to action and to the sounds of words which, when well done can make us seem that which we are not or more than we are").[4] My textual interpretant therefore suggests itself through the convergence of the descriptive systems[5] of civility and oratorical action in the context of social exchange: the face to face interaction of conversation contains the model for the interaction between dancer and spectator. Arbeau's *Orchesographie* reveals traces of the existence of a mutual awareness even though Renaissance social dance was not performed in a formal theatrical framework. For instance, Arbeau makes mention of onlookers as an audience. Some steps are to be done ". . . en regardant les assistants modestement . . ." ("glancing modestly the while at the spectators . . .")[6] and the dancer is made conscious of turning his back ". . . du cousté qu'aviez les visages" ("where the faces are").[7] He also discourages changing the traditional order of steps in the gaillard because ". . . les spectateurs se pourroient ennuyer d'attendre trop longtemps ladicte cadance" (". . . the onlookers might find it wearisome waiting so long for the cadence . . .").[8] The conventions of choreography had already engendered certain expectations which convert the otherwise casual onlooker into an audience. Furthermore, the mutual expectations of interlocutors in their social performance will reveal a strategy of interaction inherent in the dance. Such a model, however, is only possible once we ascertain the link between what Guazzo calls action and the interlocking categories of the pose and movement. It will first be necessary to determine how Guazzo places what he calls action in a rhetorical framework.

The need for action and therefore artifice in conversation is justified by Guazzo as a "natural instinct" for rhetoric: ". . . tutti gli huomini naturalmente studiano ragionando di persuadere, e di commovere . . ." (". . . all men naturally try to persuade and to move when they talk to each other . . .").[9] Since it is also natural that men improve the means to secure their instinctual needs, ". . . cosi non potrà se non essere commendato, et detto naturale il ragionamento di colui, ilquale, alle cose necesarie aggiunge qualche cosa di meglio . . ." (". . . it can only be natural and praiseworthy to add something better to the necessary things of one's speech . . .").[10] This natural evolution towards "qualche cosa di meglio" is an apology for artifice. ". . . Io vorrei, ch'egli aiutasse la natura con un poco d'arte . . ." (". . . I would like him to help nature with a little art"), says Annibale.[11] Action is that "poco d'arte" which is not found in "le midolle dell'institutioni dell'oratore" ("in the marrow of the oratorical institution") but rather "intorno alla scorza" ("around the bark").[12] Therefore, like dance movement, action is not supposed to be acquired through arduous study: "Posto, che voi non conoscete le parti di questa attione, voi conoscete però in voi questo dono, e sapete di possederlo" ("Let us suppose that you haven't learned the parts of this action: you nevertheless are aware of this gift in yourself and that you possess it").[13] At this ambiguous and yet nodal point of the text action is defined as a gift and is therefore incontrovertibly a variant of grace.

Of course, Guazzo includes both physical movement and vocal delivery in his definition of action. He speaks in general terms about the voice which has two clearly defined roles to play. First of all, the voice must incarnate measure. In this sense, it is merely an extension of posture. Precepts for the voice describe measure both as an evenness of pitch and of pace. The even pitch gives a melodic quality which Cicero called "suavis."[14] Regularity of pace or rhythmic periodicity is a function of clear pronunciation, expressed again as a "pas trop et pas trop peu."

> ANN. Le parole poi s'hanno a proferire distintamente, e a spiccare le sillabe, ma in maniera, che non paia, che si vogliano accoppiare, ò combinare insieme tutte le lettere, come sogliono i fanciulli, che apprendono a leggere, il che arreca fastidio a gli ascoltanti . . . Ma non bisogna anco affrettarle in maniera, che come cibo in bocca d'uno affamato, si divorino senza masticarle.

> ANN. One should pronounce words distinctly and separate the syllables but not in such a way that it seems we want to join all the letters together as children do who are learning to read; this bothers listeners . . . but we also shouldn't pronounce so fast that like starved people with food in their mouths, we are devouring without chewing.[15]

Guazzo, however, adds the function of diversity to the voice:

> Cav. Io non credo però, che vogliate, che nel parlare si serbi sempre un medesimo suono, e una medesima misura. ANN. Non già, perche il diletto de'ragionamenti non meno che quello della musica è cagionato dalla mutatione della voce. Anzi io voleva hora nel finire questo ragionamento ricordare, che si come scambievolmente hora stiamo in piedi, hor passeggiamo, hor seggiamo, e non possiamo lungamente patire un solo di questi siti: cosi il variare della voce acquista gratia e a guisa d'uno istromento di molte corde, apporta sollevamento all' ascoltatore, e al dicitore . . .

> Cav. But I don't think that you want us in speaking to keep one tone and one measure. ANN. Absolutely not, because the delight of conversing like that of music is based on changes in the voice. And, indeed, in order to complete this subject I might remind you that just as sometimes we are standing, then we sit, then we walk without being able to stay very long in any one manner, so the variation of the voice is graceful and like an instrument with many chords gives relief to the listener and the speaker . . .[16]

The body is circumscribed by attitudes and poses. The voice, by contrast, is described in terms of a mobility or the changes from one pose to another. Moreover, the activity of the voice has a theoretical importance for the role of motion in dance. By the same token, the theory of the pose in the dancer-spectator interaction is linked to a vocal code: silence as a suspension of speech. The reversibility of the theory of vocal functions and that of a dancer-spectator interaction is actualized in the text by means of two subsidiary codes: a financial and a medical one. Silence and speech are discussed metaphorically throughout the text as revenue and expenditure. The medical code translates revenue and expenditure into physical repose (the pose) and physical exertion (movement) or expenditure of energy and resources. It remains to show how Guazzo's text as interpretant points to the two primary effects of the dancing body. They are none other than Aristotle's first two forms of rhetorical proof: favorably disposing the spectator and convincing him of one's moral character.

B. *The Strategy of Conversing*

My use of the term strategy implies a conception of civility as politics already implicit in my previous analysis of courtesy books but which I should now render as explicit as possible. As Paolo Valesio notes, the mundane strategies of the Renaissance have nothing to do with "modern bourgeois etiquette" but engage "politics in the only concrete sense of the word": that of "everyday interactions among men."[17] The ultimate strategy of civility, and therefore of conversing, is to observe the bodies of others in order to understand and eventually manipulate them as well as to control one's own appearance to others to the same end. There are two stages in the cultivation of self-control which governs others. At the earlier stage one manipulates others by controlling oneself (following the Code) and observing others for revelatory breaches in the same Code. He who already has the power to make others dance is in an ideal position to observe.[18] In the second and more advanced stage, in controlling oneself one controls others because everything one does is imitated by others. At this stage the gestural Code coincides with genius, inspiration or even vice as Montaigne explains in "de l'incommodité de la grandeur" ("of the disadvantage of greatness"):

> Comme on leur cede [aux grands] tous avantages d'honneur, aussi conforte l'on et auctorise les deffauts et vices qu'ils ont, non seulement par approbation, mais aussi par l'imitation. Chacun des suyvans d'Alexandre portoit comme luy la teste à costé . . .

As we yield to them all the advantages of honor, so we confirm and
authorize the defects and vices they have, not only by approbation but
also by imitation. Every one of the followers of Alexander carried his
head on one side, as he did . . . [19]

There is a narcissistic sense to the conformism of civility. Conformity for
the one who is the ideal model is seeing oneself in others. However, in order
to become the model one must first gain others' esteem. The quest for
esteem—glory, reputation, honor—must also be dissimulated by modesty,
deferentiality; in short, an appearance of goodness bordering on if not
synonymous with virtue and piety. The reverence, having served as an
example that civility and dance were not discontinuous, also affords an
example of the political strategy of civility. Montaigne called all reverences
"ceremonies" or artificial gestures ". . . par où on acquiert, le plus souvent à
tort, l'honneur d'estre bien humble et courtois: on peut estre humble de
gloire" (". . . by which men gain credit most often wrongfully, for being very
humble and courteous; a man may be humble through vainglory").[20] In the
reverence between equals, reputation, seemingly bestowed on the addressee,
is actually predicated of the addressor. He who appears to humble himself
acquires a position of superiority. "Comme le donner est qualité ambitieuse
et de prerogative, aussi est l'accepter qualité de summission" ("As giving is
an ambitious quality and a prerogative, so is accepting a quality of
submission").[21] In other words, the positions of superiority and submission
are both reversed and dissimulated.

Guazzo's exposition of conversing reveals the strategic roles of the
pose and movement in dancing: the role of the pose is to dispose others
favorably to us; the role of movement is to prove goodness of character.
These proofs are effected simultaneously; one can never be sure where one
ends and the other begins. Pose and movement, like silence and speech,
both alternate and interpenetrate each other: their independence is only an
artificial convenience of analysis.

Il Cavalier Guglielmo remarks that social intercourse, understood
throughout the text as conversation, is dominated by ". . . il desiderio di
conservare, e di aumentar la facultà, e d'aggrandir l'esser suo, [che] non
lascia stare le persone con le mani a cintola . . ." (". . . the desire to conserve
and increase their means and increase their state, [which] doesn't leave
time for people to be idle").[22] This is borne out by the fact that ". . . non si
discorre d'altro, che di comperare, di vendere, di permutare, di dare, ò di
torre danari ad interesse . . ." (". . . people speak of nothing but buying,
selling, bartering, giving or taking money with interest").[23] Annibale
outlines a theory of the virtues of civil conversing as a means of acquiring
wealth and its prerequisite, the favor and good will of others:

> Io propongo la conversatione . . . perche nel conversare si apprendano i
> buoni costumi, e le virtù, per mezzo delle quali si dispensino, e si
> conservino drittamente i beni della fortuna, e si venga ad acquistare il
> favore, la benivolenza, e la gratia altrui.

> I propose conversation . . . because in it we learn the good manners and
> virtues through which windfalls are properly obtained and conserved
> and by which one acquires the favor, good will and grace of others.[24]

Annibale speaks as a philosopher, elaborating a theory of conversation, and
as a doctor as well, applying his discourse thoughtfully to the case of the
convalescent Guglielmo, counseling him on sickness and health. The
medical code transforms the transaction from untutored youth to civil
gentleman into a movement from illness to health. In this manner, the
materialism of civility's financial code is attenuated. The drive to wealth is
represented retroactively as a metaphor for health. Annibale recommends
the solitary Guglielmo engage in conversing as a kind of cure. Conversing,
however, is only curative if it is enriching: "Stando che il solitario sia
infermo, come habbiamo detto, io propongo per la sua salute, che egli procuri
conversando, che per buono spatio di tempo si maggiore l'entrata, che la
spesa di casa sua" ("Let us say that the solitary man is sick, as we have
indicated, I propose that he engage in conversation for his health so that for
a good period of time the income of the house is greater than the
expenditure").[25] In other words, one is "enriched"as a listener but
"impoverished" as a speaker. the convergence of the two series of
polarities, silence/speech and revenue/expenditure occurs within the two
signifiers: "orrechie" and "lingua" ("ears" and "tongue"):

> Ann. Dimandato un savio huomo per qual cagione ci havesse la natura
> date due orrechie, e una sola lingua; perche, rispose, siano piu quelle
> cose, che s'odano, che quelle, che si parlino. Questa risposta m'ha
> datto sogetto d'attribuire all'orrechie l'entrata, e alla lingua la spesa. Et
> perche io sia meglio inteso, dico, che nel conversare e necessario l'uso
> di due cose principali, che sono la lingua, e i costumi, onde a queste due
> parti rivolgeremo il nostro pensiero.

> Ann. As a wise man was asked why nature has given us two ears and
> only one tongue he replied because we should hear more than we speak.
> That answer gave me reason to attribute income to the ears and
> expenditure to the tongue. And that I might be better understood, I say
> that two things are necessary in conversation principally, which are the
> tongue and manners, therefore I will address my thought to these two
> matters.[26]

Thus, expenditure, whose agent is the tongue, is opposed to income whose agents are the ears, replaced at the end of this passage by "i costumi" ("manners"). "I costumi" ("moeurs") in the sixteenth century signifies both the "honnête extérieur," becoming manners ("contenance extérieure" or "comportement") and also moral quality ("qualità," "disposition et naturel" or "complexion").[27] Since "orrechie" are annexed by the category of "costumi" as the text indicates, silence gains more importance than speech. Indeed, Annibale implies that "i costumi" subsume the two poles of conversation:

> Cavalie. Et perche volete voi ristringervi solamente a queste due? Ann. Perche, se voi considerate bene, noi principalmente acquistiamo nelle conversationi la benivolenza altrui con le maniere del ragionare e con la qualità de'costumi. Anzi io potrei ad un certo modo, ridurre tutta la conversatione sotto il capo de'costumi . . . Nondimeno perche vi sono alcune parti della lingua, lequali non dipendono in tutto dai costumi, io seguirò questi due capi.

> Cav. And why do you want to restrict yourself to these two parts? Ann. Because, if you consider well, in conversation we ascertain the benevolence of others principally through our way of discussing and the quality of our manners. So in a certain way I could reduce all conversation under the head of manners . . . Nevertheless since there are some parts of language ["lingua"] which do not depend completely on manners ["costumi"], I will pursue these two subjects.[28]

Income ("orrechie") which, as "costumi," almost replaces "lingua" in conversation, is therefore a technique of silent and sympathetic attention accorded to the interlocutor. This technique has its rules. In listening, it is necessary ". . . [che] si guardi dall'asprezza de gli occhi, da itorcimenti della persona, dall'intensa gravità delle ciglia, dalla tristezza del volto, da riguardarsi attorno . . ." (". . . [that one] avoid a harsh expression in the eyes, twisting the body, a frowning seriousness, looking around . . .").[29] In short, all the precepts of posture are operative. Silence is also a technique inasmuch as it is not natural.

> Essendo adunque il tacere, e l'udire delle cose piu difficili, che siano al mondo, bisogna, che'l nostro infermo si disponga di raffrenare questo suo appetito, e facendo resistenza a se stesso, habituarsi pian piano a tener più chiusa la bocca, e più aperte l'orrechie . . .

> Since being silent and listening is one of the hardest things in the world to do, our sick man should prepare himself to rein in his appetite, and resisting his own impulse, slowly get used to keeping his mouth more closed and his ears more open . . .[30]

Silence is income because a good listener pleases others and disposes them favorably. Annibale:

> . . . il che egli non farà cosi tosto, come s'accorgerà, che nelle conversationi s'acquista la benivolenza, e la gratia altrui non meno ascoltando gratiosamente, che ragionando piacevolmente, perche noi ci chiamiamo obligati a coloro, che sono attenti alle nostre parole . . .

> . . . which thing he will no sooner do, than he will realize, that the benevolence and the good grace of others is acquired not less by listening graciously than by discussing pleasantly, since we consider ourselves obliged to those who are attentive to our words . . .[31]

Therefore, silence and the pose put the spectator in a favorable frame of mind.

While silence may be the gentleman's chief concern, he is nevertheless obliged to speak by the silence of others. The expenditure of speech is not without its own income since speaking itself is profitable:

> Come quel danaio, che è bene speso, oltre al profitto di chi lo riceve, torna a commodo di chi lo sborsa; cosi le parole ben considerate reccano beneficio a chi le ascolta, e honore a chi le esprime. Et si come fuori d'una borsa escono diverse sorti di moneta o d'oro, o d'argento, o di rame, cosi fuori della bocca escono sentenze, e altre parole di più, e di manco valore.

> Just as money which is well spent besides being of profit to him who receives it, also profits the one who spends it, so well-received words bring profit to the listener and honor to the speaker. And just as different sorts of money come out of a purse, some gold, some silver and some copper, so sentences issue from the mouth and other words of more or less value.[32]

Speech can produce good or ill effects, but the art of speaking well within the system of civility is not limited to avoiding injurious or infelicitous phrases ("parole . . . di manco valore"). The give and take of conversation is not income and expenditure: the framework of exchange is debt:

> Ma non havranno interamente pagato il debito, se non cercano insieme di giovare, e di dilettare, acciohe raccolgano tutto il frutto della lingua . . . . Chi desidera adunque usar felicemente della civil conversatione, ha da considerare, che la lingua è lo specchio, e'l ritratto dell'animo suo; e che si come dal suono del danaio conosciamo la bontà, e falsità sua, cosi dal suono delle parole comprendiamo a dentro la qualità dell'huomo, e i suoi costumi.

But we will not have entirely paid the debt if we do not strive at once
both to profit and to please so that we draw in all the fruit of language . . .
Whoever wishes therefore to use civil conversation to the happiest end
should consider that language ["la lingua"] is the mirror and portrait of
our soul; and just as we recognize the authenticity or the falsity of
money from its sound, so from the sounds of words we understand the
quality of the man within and his morals ["costumi"].[33]

The framework of exchange is a mutual debt incurred successively by each
party at the moment that words are uttered. Montaigne called this mutual
debt a "subtile science" made up of a "bien-faict" and a "recognoissance."[34] The
debt to which Annibale refers is first of all a negative one: do not offend the
other: "Quelli per tanto, che aspirano al grado della virtù, e che vogliono
esser degni della civil conversatione, hanno sopra tutto a guardarsi di non
offendere altrui con la lingua" ("Those however who aspire to virtue and
want to be worthy of civil conversation have above all to avoid offending
others in speaking").[35] Speech can only "pay the debt," be a "bien-faict" if
it is in a currency of the highest value: of a rhetorical value (gold): "Dunque
se volete, che si muovano gli affetti, e si persuadano gli animi altrui, con la
lingua, non potete di manco, che non ricorriate ai precetti della Retorica . . ."
("So that if you want to move the emotions of men and persuade the minds
of others, with speech, you cannot but have recourse to the precepts of
Rhetoric . . .").[36] The action of the voice is "gold" in that it bespeaks value,
reflects on its possessor as a man of worth (in the objective and subjective
sense of this genitive) and solicits the profit of esteem or glory: the
"recognoissance."

   To sum up, the use of "lingua" does not include words as units of
meaning but rather as units of vocal gesture. In conversation the emotional
response of the listener precedes the reception of the message. The silent
sympathy of the other favorably disposes while the concomitant desire to
ingratiate oneself is both dissimulated and consummated by the voice's
sound alone: ". . . come dal suono del danaio conosciamo la bontà, e falsità
sua, cosi dal suono delle parole comprendiamo a dentro la qualità
dell'huomo, e i suoi costumi." Value (rhetorical or monetary) is not
demonstrated by argumentation, nor, in coins, by the marks of public use
and authority.[37] "Car comme *nature* a donné de certaines marques à l'*or*
pour connaître s'il est faux: ainsi a-t-elle voulu que sa conversation fît
connaître son naturel et ses moeurs" ("Just as *nature* has given certain
marks to *gold* so that we may tell if it is false, so she has ordained that his
conversation reveal his character and morals").[38] The diversity or variety of
the voice, in short, its mobility, manifests distinguishing marks which
function as a deixis of value. Likewise, in the dance, movement performs the

proof of "goodness" which both dissimulates the clandestine appeal to the emotions of the first proof and yields the "profit" of power over others: glory.[39] The voice transforms our financial code into a numismatic one. However, this numismatics, the metaphor of the voice as gold coin, situates value (understood both as moral goodness and credit) within an economic sphere devoid of fixed authority. Like the term "virtu" in the corpus of texts under discussion, "valore" is a term which can signify goodness in the metaphysical sense or goodness in the most general and generic sense of the term as would the Latin "virtus." Furthermore, value and deixis of value become interchangeable in such a system. In order to illustrate ". . . cette condition de vivre par la relation à autruy . . ." (". . . this disposition to live with reference to others . . ."), Montaigne described value as a function of credit dependent on display. His economic metaphor supplies a useful illustration: ". . . si qu'aux uns liars valent escuz, aux autres le rebours, le monde estimant l'emploicte [la dépense] de la valeur selon la montre" (". . . for some, farthings are worth crowns, for the others the reverse, since the world judges expense and means according to the show").[40] The recognition of value is immediate, aesthetic rather than intellectual, just as the sound a coin makes when dropped is associated with its alloys. Both the sound of words and gold must "ring" true. In other terms, the protocol for an interaction is established without the institution of conventional signs, vocal or physical, as representations of a scale of value. By the same token, the dancing body was not a subject of discourse on dance because the physical indications of "goodness" were floating signifiers: their signified vacillated between an absolute and a fiduciary concept of value.

The approaches to historical gestuality suggested by gestural semiotics seem hampered by the problematic absence of a linguistic model. Gestural semiotics is particularly impeded with regard to the archeology of social practices. Without the possibilities of direct observation, the semiotic enterprise is caught between the insufficiences of a linguistic model and the unavailability of a new model based on an autonomous system of notation.[41] Therefore, I have preferred a method which applies textual semiotics to the "empire of illusions" of transmissible knowledge, to the codes and descriptive systems of treatises, while remaining aware of the limitations imposed by the body as referent. As far as possible I have tried to accommodate the literarity of treatises, their network of metaphors, with the literality of the body as an instrument. I have sought neither to prejudge the prerogatives of history nor those of language: that is to say I have not homologized the dance with language, nor have I collapsed the referent into a pure play of signifiers.

If a semiotics of dance is impossible in the Renaissance it is precisely because, despite the inherently ideological character of its strategy, gesture cuts across the previsions of choreography and forces us to radically reconsider the sense of codification in dance during this period. Just as the musical notation to be found in the tabulatures of dance manuals consists of a tenor or canto fermo theme upon which musicians accompanying the dance would improvise, creating the polyphony of a second melody or descant, so gesture can also be considered as a "discantus supra librum" ("a descanting on the book"), a truly fantasmatic body of polyphonic movement, creating a choreographic descant on the canto fermo of choreographic notation.

NOTES

Chapter One

[1]A historical and critical examination of early dance reconstructions and the archeological impulse in theater in the last 150 years is the projected subject of a separate study.

[2]See her remarks on the Ballo-Pantomime in "Die Choreographie der Hoftänze in Burgund, Frankreich und Italien im 15. Jahrhundert" (Diss. Göttingen Phil. Fak. of Georg August Universität 1956), p. 188. This unpublished dissertation will be hereafter referred to as Brainard, *Chor.*

[3]Thoinot Arbeau, *Orchesographie. Et traicte en Forme de Dialogue, par lequel toutes personnes peuvent facilement apprendre et practiquer l'honneste exercice des dances* (Lengres: Jehan des preyz, 1589; rpt. Bologna: Forni Editore, 1969), p. 4[r]. I have referred to Mary Stuart Evans' English translation of *Orchesography* but have frequently emended it to render a more exact equivalent of the French original. I will, however, supply references throughout to the edition edited by Julia Sutton (New York: Dover Publications, 1967), p. 14. It will be referred to hereafter as *Evans.*

[4]See Arthur Michel, *Die Ältesten Tanzlehrbücher* (Brunn: Rudolf M. Rohrer, n.d.) published in English as "The Earliest Dance-Manuals," in *Medievalia et Humanistica* 3 (1945), pp. 117-131; see also Ingrid Brainard, "The Role of the Dancing Master in Fifteenth Century Courtly Society," in *Fifteenth Century Studies* 2 (1979), pp. 21-44. Transcriptions of these treatises are as follows: Dante Bianchi, "Un trattato inedito di Domenico da Piacenza," in *La Bibliofilia* LXV (1963), pp. 109-149; C. Mazzi, "Il 'libro dell'arte del danzare' di Antonio Cornazano," in *La Bibliofilia* XVII (1915), pp. 1-50; an English translation of Cornazano is now available as *The Book on the Art of Dancing*, trans. Madeleine Inglehearn and Peggy Forsyth (London: Dance Books Ltd., 1981). The different editions of Guglielmo Ebreo da Pesaro's manuscripts are too numerous to list here. Suffice it to mention that the Dance Collection, Library and Museum of the Performing Arts at Lincoln Center, The New York Public Library, holds *Ghuglielmj ebreij pisauriensis depraticha seuarte vulghare opusculum* in the Cia Fornaroli Collection.

[5]For a general description of the content of these treatises, see Otto Kinkeldey, *A Jewish Dancing Master of the Renaissance: Guglielmo Ebreo* (New York: Dance Horizons, 1972). For a detailed analysis of the steps see Ingrid Brainard, *The Art of Courtly Dancing in the Early Renaissance* (West Newton, Mass.: I.G. Brainard, 1981). This work is to a large degree a re-working in English of parts of *Chor.* Its format is that of an instruction manual for reconstructors in which many of the details of the earlier research do not reappear.

[6]Thoinot Arbeau is an anagramatic pseudonym for Jehan Tabourot. For more information on Arbeau see André Mary, " *'L'Orchésographie'* de Thoinot Arbeau," in *Les Trésors des Bibliothèques de France*, ed. E. Dacier (Paris, 1935), V, 85-99 and Peirre Perrenet, *Etienne Tabourot, sa famille et son temps* (Dijon: 1926).

[7]Cervera, Arxiu Historic, Fonds notarial, 3,3. (1496?). A facsimile of part of this work can be found in Capmany, *Folklore y Costumbres de España*, ed. F. Carrerar y Candi (Barcelona, 1934), I, vii. The *Tarragó Ms.* Barcelona, Bibl. Central-Hospital de la Santa Creu. A facsimile can be found in F. Pujol and J. Amades, *Cançoner popular de Catalunya* (Barcelona: 1936). See also Francine Lancelot, "L'Ecriture de la danse: le système Feuillet," in *Ethnologie Française* (1971), tome I, numéro 1, p. 29.

[8]The "bal de la reine de cessile" is in the manuscript collection of the Bibliothèque Nationale, Paris, f. fr. 5699 (Guillaume Cousinot's *Gestes des noblese francoyse*) and is published in A. Vallet de Viriville, *Chronique de la Pucelle* (Paris: 1859), pp. 99-103. Ernest Closson published a facsimile of the Brussels manuscript, *Le Manuscrit dit des Basses Danses de la Bibliothèque de Bourgogne* (Geneva: Minkoff Reprint, 1976); the Toulouze treatise is reprinted as Michel Toulouze, *L'Art et Instruction de Bien Dancer* (Printed for the Royal College of Physicians of London. 1936); Robert Copelande, *The manner to dance Bace dances* (London: Pear Tree Press, 1937); Antonius de Arena, *Ad Suos Compagnones, qui sont de persona friantes, bassas Dansas et Branlos practicantes novellos perquamplurimos mandat* (Paris: Chez Philippes Gaultier, 1533). Daniel Heartz dates the first edition of Arena as 1529 while maintaining that the treatise was written ten years earlier while the author was a student at Avignon. See his introduction to the Attaignant collection, v. 2, pp. XXXI-LIV. The choreographies of the Moderne collection (*Plusieurs basses danses*) are reproduced in François Lesure, "Danses et chansons à danser au début du XVIe siècle," in *Receuil de Travaux offert à M. Clovis Brunel* (Paris: 1955). There are two sixteenth-century collections containing the music for basse dances: Pierre Attaignant, *Preludes, chansons and dances* (Paris: 1529-1530; Neuilly-sur-Seine: Société de Musique d'Autrefois, 1964) v. 2, containing eighteen basse dances which the editor D. Heartz describes as the first polyphonic dances in France; Stribaldi, Turin, Archivio di Stato, Biscaretti, Mazzo 4, no. 14, basse danse scroll, dated 1517, edited in Paul Meyer, "Rôle de chansons à danser du XVI siècle," in *Romania* XXIII (1894), pp. 156-160; see also Adrian Le Roy, *Premier Livre de tabulature de luth* (1551) and *Fantaisies et Danses* (Instruction de 1568); rpt. Le Choeur des Muses, C.N.R.S., 1960 and 1962 as well as the four-volume book of "danseries" by Jean d'Estrées, 1551-1558. To consult much of this material see Frederick Crane, *Materials for the Study of the 15th-Century Basse Dance* (Rome: American Institute of Musicology. Studies and Documents 16, 1968). For a collation of the steps of the Brussels Ms. with Toulouuze's *L'Art et Instruction* see James L. Jackman, *Fifteenth Century Basse Dances* (Wellesley College: 1964). For a fairly comprehensive bibliography of pre-classical dance treatises see Margaret M. McGowan, "La pratique de la danse au XVIe siècle," in her *L'Art du Ballet de Cour en France, 1581-1643* (Paris: C.N.R.S., 1978), pp. 29-47. See also W. Thomas Marrocco, *Inventory of Fifteenth Century Bassedanze, Balli and Balletti* (New York: Congress on Research in Dance, 1981) and Ingrid Brainard, "Bassedanse, Bassadanza and Ballo in the Fifteenth Century," in the *Proceedings of the Second Conference on Research in Dance* (New York: CORD, 1970), pp. 64-79.

[9]Domenico da Piacenza. Paris, Bibliothèque Nationale, f. it. 972, fol. 4. The title by which this treatise is known, *De arte saltandi et choreas ducendi* is a later addition. Translations from fifteenth-century Italian treatises are mine throughout unless otherwise indicated.

[10]Selma Jeanne Cohen asks where the reality of a piece of choreography lies, an identity necessarily distinct from its performances and yet which makes demands on those performances while tolerating a wide variety of alterations which do not compromise its identity. See her *Next Week, Swan Lake. Reflections on Dance and Dances* (Middletown: Wesleyan University Press, 1982). In what follows I consider the invariant identity of the basse dance (which I write in English in order to translate both the French and Italian) and therefore its universal recognizability to be attributable to a theoretical body conceived of as dancing it correctly. This theoretical body which it is the task of this study to describe emerged as exemplary to the European consciousness of formalized social behavior devolving from the courts.

[11]Brainard, *Chor.*, p. 20. Translations from this work are mine throughout. Ambrosio writes that French dances were praticed in Italy in the fifteenth century: "Et li foro facti bally

francesi con madonna duchessa et con madonna Lionora in meçço del pasto proprio." Cited in McGowan, *L'Art du Ballet de Cour,* p. 30.

[12]Brainard, *Chor.,* pp. 1-8.

[13]She speaks of the sixteenth century as "a time which knows the authentic basse dance almost only through hearsay and no longer possesses the physical sense of its style." Ibid., p. 47, note 3. For McGowan, on the other hand, Arbeau's basse danse is more sophisticated and complex than the fifteenth-century examples (op. cit., p. 30).

[14]See, in particular, Michel Guilcher, "L'interprétation de l'orchésographie par des danseurs et des musiciens d'aujourd'hui," in *La Recherche en Danse* 2 (1983), pp. 21-32.

[15]Norbert Elias writes, ". . . there is ample evidence to show that at this period customs, behavior and fashions from the court are continuously penetrating the upper middle classes . . ." Indeed, Elias bases his theory of the civilizing process in part on this phenomenon. See his *The History of Manners* (New York: Pantheon, 1982), pp. 100-101. See also H. de la Fontaine Verwey, "The first 'book of etiquette' for children: Erasmus' 'De civilitate morum puerilium,' " in *Quaerendo,* 1 (1971), pp. 19-30.

[16]Castiglione's *Il Cortegiano* appears in Italy in 1528 and is translated into French in 1537. Della Casa's 1558 *Galateo* appears in French in 1562 and the year of the publication of Stefano Guazzo's *La Civil Conversatione,* 1574, witnesses two French translations, one by Chappuys, the other by Belleforest. For further information consult Mario Richter, *Giovanni Della Casa in Francia nel secolo XVI* (Rome: Edizioni di Storia e Letteratura, 1966), pp. 53-85 and John Leon Lievsay, *Stefano Guazzo and the English Renaissance, 1575-1675* (Chapel Hill: the University of North Carolina Press, 1961).

[17]"In its luxurious gatherings the Burgundian court seems to forshadow the brilliant events of the sixteenth-century French court." Georges Doutrepont, *La Litterature française à la cour des Ducs de Bourgogne* (Paris: Honoré Champion, 1909), p. 517.

[18]The ornamentation of the *doppio,* consisting in *ondeggiare* and *campeggiare* which I will discuss in chapter four, is none other for Brainard than the *pas double* described in the Brussels Ms. and by Toulouze and Copelande: "A lifting onto the toes for the first part of the step and a sinking onto the whole foot for the last part." Brainard, *Chor.,* pp. 239-240.

[19]Brainard refers to a "wirklich erstaunliche Übereinstimmung" ("a really astounding correspondence") between the *Orchesographie* and Domenico's dance treatise which opens the way to a direct road between sixteenth-century dance technique and the fifteenth century Italian steps (". . . weil sie einen direkten Weg von der Tanztechnik des 16. Jahrhunderts zu den gewöhnlich so schwer fassbaren Tanzschritten des Quattrocento eröffnet . . ."). *Chor.,* pp. 300-301.

[20]Ibid., p. 42.

[21]Arbeau clearly does not use *maniera,* yet almost no arm or hand movements are given by him while he does prescribe their use, notably in the *pavane d'Espagne* and in many *branles.*

[22]This is also indicated by the text. "Capriol. Je prevoy donq que nostre posterité sera ignorante de toutes ces nouvelles dances que venez de nommer, par les mesmes causes qui nous ont oste la cognoissance de celles de nos anciens . . . Monsieur arbeau ne permectez cela de vostre pouvoir puisque pouvez remedier: mectez en quelque chose par escript cela sera cause que j'apprendray ceste civilité . . . Vray est que vostre methode d'escripre est telle, qu'en vostre absence, sur vos theoriques et preceptes, un disciple pourra seul en sa chambre apprendre vos enseignements" ("I foresee then that posterity will remain ignorant of all these new dances you have named for the same reason that we have been deprived of the knowledge of those of our ancestors . . . Do not allow this to happen, Monsieur Arbeau, as it is within your power to prevent it. Set these things down in writing to enable me to learn this 'civilité' . . . In truth, your method of writing is such that a pupil, by following your theory and precepts, even

in your absence, could teach himself in the seclusion of his own chamber"). Arbeau, *Orch.,* pp. 5v-5r; *Evans,* p. 15.

[23]Ibid., p. 25v; *Evans,* p. 51 (my emphasis). What smacks of utopia for the sixteenth century is the collocation of dance and "honnestêté." Arbeau's reconstruction of old dances is meant to counteract the corruption of the present. "Je le veulx bien pour le désir que j'ay que telles dances honnestes soient remises au dessus, en lieu des dances lascives et deshontées que l'on a introduit en leur place au regret des sages seigneurs et des dames et matrones de bon et pudique jugement" ("I shall do so willingly, in the hope that such honourable dances are reinstated and replace the lascivious, shameless ones introduced in their stead to the regret of wise lords and ladies and matrons of sound and chaste judgment"). Ibid., p. 30v; *Evans,* p. 59.

[24]See, for example, Béranger de la Tour d'Albennas, *Choréide, Autrement, Louenge du bal* (Lyons, 1556) and Sir John Davies, *Orchestra or, A Poem of Dancing,* ed. E.V.W. Tillyard (1594; rpt. New York: Dance Horizons, n.d.); see also James L. Miller, "Choreia: Visions of the Cosmic Dance in Western Literature from Plato to Jean de Meun," (Diss. Toronto, 1979).

[25]Michel de Montaigne, *Essais* (Paris: Garnier, 1962), II, XII, pp. 498-499. "What of the eyebrows? What of the shoulders? There is no movement that does not speak both a language intelligible without instruction, and a public language; which means, seeing the variety and particular use of other languages, that this one must rather be judged the one proper to human nature. I omit what necessity teaches privately and promptly to those who need it, and the finger alphabets, and the grammars in gestures, and the sciences which are practiced and expressed only by gestures, and the nations which Pliny says have no other language." *The Complete Essays of Montaigne,* trans. Donald M. Frame (Stanford: Stanford University Press, 1965), p. 332. All translations of Montaigne will come from this edition and will be referred to in notes as *Frame.*

[26]"We must return to that basic given: the body, such as it has been invented by legalistic procedure. This discovery is not realized and has never been made historically once and for all. It surfaces as an aesthetic statement or by deflection of the myth through technical knowledge." Pierre Legendre, *La Passion d'être un Autre. Etude pour la Danse* (Paris: Seuil, 1978), p. 154 (my translation).

[27]". . . as for movements, knowledge of dance in itself seems to have been the least of the dancer's occupations." E. Rodocanachi, "La Danse en Italie du XV au XVII siècle," in *La Revue des études historiques* (nov.-dec., 1905), p. 574 (my translation).

[28]Jacques Amyot, *Project de l'Eloquence Royale, composé pour Henry III, roi de France* (Versailles: chez Lamy, 1805), p.51 (my translation).

[29]See Marc Angenot, "Les traités de l'éloquence du corps," in *Semiotika,* VIII (1973), pp. 60-82. See also *XVIIe Siècle (Rhétorique du Geste et de la Voix à l'Age Classique)* (Juillet-Septembre 1981), N°. 132, 33e année, n° 3.

[30]François Rabelais, *Oeuvres Complètes* (Paris: Gallimard, 1955), ch. XIX, pp. 254-258.

[31]"Mental illness doesen't exist in the classical period if one understands it to mean the natural environment of the insane, the mediation between the madman one sees and the dementia to be analyzed, in short the link of the insane to his madness. The madman and his insanity are foreign to one another; the truth of each is reserved to them separately and as if confiscated to a place within themselves." Michel Foucault, *Histoire de la Folie à l'âge classique* (Paris: Gallimard, 1972), p. 223 (my translation).

[32]Daniel Heartz, "The Basse Dance. Its Evolution circa 1450 to 1550," in *Annales Musicologigues. Môyen Age et Renaissance,* T. VI (1958-1963), pp. 287-340.

[33]Ibid., p. 326. Rabelais' use of the term "matrone" in phrases such as "pudicques

matrones" and "pudicité matronale" ("chaste matrons" and "matronly modesty") indicate that the term "matrone" referred to a married lady, and thus to a paragon of feminine virtue, rather than to age as such. See *Gargantua,* chs. 9 and 56.

[34]"Syllepsis," in *Critical Inquiry* (Summer 1980), vol. 6, no. 4, p. 627.

[35]Ibid. See also, Riffaterre, "La trace de l'intertexte," in *La Pensée* 215 (October 1980), pp. 14-15: "La signifiance . . . n'est donc ni dans le texte ni dans l'intertexte, mais à mi-chemin des deux, dans l'interprétant, qui dicte au lecteur la manière de les voir, de les comparer, de les interpréter par conséquent dans leur inséparabilité même." ("Significance . . . is therefore neither in the text nor the intertext, but half way between the two, in the interpretant, which dictates the way to see them, to compare them and consequently to interpret them in their very inseparability.") My translation.

[36]Frances Yates points out that although Quintilian's *Institutio* was known to the Middle Ages through incomplete copies the text was rediscovered in its entirety in 1416. See *The Art of Memory* (Chicago: University of Chicago Press, 1966), p. 56.

Chapter II

[1]Arbeau, *Orch.,* p. 6v; *Evans.,* p. 16.

[2]Quintilian, *The Institutio Oratoria of Quintilian* (London: William Heinemann Ltd.: Cambridge, Mass: Harvard University Press, 1969), XI, III (82), p. 289.

[3]Ibid., (159), p. 331. The striking similarities between the orator's and the gentleman's posture will be borne out in chapter 4. Quintilian also limits motion to ". . . forward, to right or left and up or down." Circular motion is ". . . faulty when applied to gesture." Ibid., (105), p. 299.

[4]Ibid., XI, III (65), p. 279. See also Aristotle, *"Art" of Rhetoric* (Cambridge: Harvard University Press, 1975), III, I, 1 (1403b), p. 347.

[5]Quintilian, op. cit. (106), p. 301.

[6]Semic selection refers to the choice of semes constituting the ground of the metaphor or the basis of the comparison underlying it. The ground is, in other terms, the common unit of meaning permitting us to compare the tenor (dance) with the vehicle (rhetoric). See Michel Le Guern, *Sémantique de la métaphore et de la métonymie* (Paris: Larousse, 1973), p. 41.

[7]Aristotle, op. cit., I, II, 3 (1358b), p. 33 (my emphasis).

[8]Ibid., I, I, 1 (1355b), p. 13.

[9]Cf. ibid., I, II, 2 (1357a), p. 25.

[10]Ibid., III, I, 1 (1404a), p. 347.

[11]Ibid., I, II, 2 (1856b), pp. 21-23.

[12]Quintilian, op. cit., XI, III (85), p. 289.

[13]Ibid., (72), p. 283.

[14]Ibid., (122), p. 309.

[15]"Its importance in oratory is sufficiently clear from the fact that there are many things which it can express without the assistance of words. For we can indicate our will not merely by a gesture of the hands, but also with a nod from the head: signs take the place of language in the dumb, and the movements of the dance are frequently full of meaning, and appeal to the emotions without any aid from words." Quintilian, op. cit., XI, III (66), p. 279.

[16]Ibid., I, XI (19), p. 191.

[17]Ibid., XI, III (88), p. 291. See also: I, XII (14), p. 199: ". . . nor need he be a finished actor in his delivery or a dancer in his gesture." Dance for Quintilian is actually a form of pantomime. For the dancer it is appropriate to use gestures which "indicate things by means of

mimicry." Oratorical action, on the other hand, requires gestures "such as naturally proceed from us simultaneously with our words." XI, III (88), p. 291. See Gaston Boissier, *De la Signification des mots Saltare et Cantare Tragoediam* (Paris: Didier, 1861).

[18]Ernst Robert Curtius, *European Literature and the Latin Middle Ages* (Princeton: Princeton University Press, 1973), p. 77. I use the term expression reservedly as the issue of expressivity is not, in my view, germane to Renaissance social dance given the dominance of the rhetorical over the pantomimic model of theatricality adopted from Roman antiquity.

[19]Aristotle, op. cit., I, II, 2 (1356a), p. 17.

[20]Quintilian, op. cit., XI, III (154), p. 329.

[21]Ibid., XII, X (43), p. 475.

[22]Ibid., III, IV (13), p. 395.

[23]Ibid.

[24]"There are also three aims which the orator must always have in view; he must instruct, move and charm. ["... ut doceat, moveat, delectet ..."] his hearers." Quintilian, op. cit., III, V (2), p. 397.

[25]Ibid., III, IV (6), p. 393.

[26]"Si vero in ostentationem comparetur declamatio, sane paulum aliquid inclinare ad voluptatem audientium debemus." The translator's use of "even" for "vero" is misleading here. It should translate to "in truth."

[27]Ibid., II, X (11), p. 277.

[28]Ibid., XI, III (154), p. 329 (my emphasis).

[29]Ibid.

[30]Ibid., VI, II (6), pp. 419-421.

[31]Arbeau, *Orch.*, p. 5v; *Evans.*, pp. 16-17.

[32]"The sole purpose of the *exordium* is to prepare our audience in such a way that they will be disposed to lend a ready ear to the rest of our speech." Quintilian, op. cit., IV, I (5), p. 9. "... In the peroration we may give full rein to our emotions, place fictitious speeches in the mouths of our characters, call the dead to life, and produce the wife or children of the accused in court..." Ibid. (28), p. 21. "The peroration... consists of appeals to the emotions... a task... of stirring the emotions of the judges, and of moulding and transforming them to the attitude which we desire." Ibid., VI, II (2), p. 417.

[33]Ibid., VI, I (26), pp. 399-401.

[34]Although the notion of a secret charm is more inherent to Quintilian's conception of rhetoric than to Aristotle's it is not part of my problematic to ascertain the true nature of rhetorical persuasion. Such an enquiry is implied by Ricoeurs' research in rhetoric. "The question that sets this project in motion is the following: what does it mean to persuade? What distinguishes persuasion from flattery, from seduction, from threat - that is to say, from the subtlest forms of violence? What does it mean, 'to influence through discourse'? To pose these questions is to decide that one cannot transform the arts of discourse into techniques without submitting them to a radical philosophical reflection outlining the concept of 'that which is persuasive' (*to pithanon*). Paul Ricoeur, *The Rule of Metaphor*, trans. Robert Czerny (Toronto and Buffalo: University of Toronto Press, 1977), p. 11.

[35]Blaise Pascal, *Pensées* (Paris: Hachette, 1971), section V, 332, pp. 483-484 (my translation).

[36]Quintilian, op. cit., VI, I (30), pp. 401-403 (my emphasis).

[37]Ibid., II, XV (6), p. 303.

[38]"... Proof is a sort of demonstration, since we are most strongly convinced when we suppose anything to have been demonstrated." Aristotle, op. cit., I, I, 11 (1355a), p. 9.

[39]Quintilian, op. cit., V, I (1), p. 157.

[40]Ibid., (2).

[41]Aristotle, op. cit., I, I, 2 (1355b), p. 15.

[42]Ibid., I, II, 2 (1357b), p. 27.

[43]Ibid.

[44]Quintilian, op. cit., V, IX, p. 195. Cf. also, ibid., V, X (12), p. 209: "We may regard as certainties, first, those things which we perceive by the senses, things for instance that we hear or see, such as signs or indications . . ."

[45]Ibid., IV, II (64), p. 85. Visibility is probably a better translation than palpability. We should be careful to avoid confusing ἐνάργεια with ἐνέργεια.

[46]Ibid., VI, II (3), pp. 435-437.

[47]Ibid., XI, III (89), p. 291.

[48]Ibid. "Non in *demonstrandis* locis ac personis adverbiorum atque pronomium obtineret vicem?" (my emphasis).

[49]". . . A certain semblance of proof is at times required by speeches composed entirely for display." Ibid., III, VII (4), p. 467.

[50]Edmond Huguet, *L'Evolution du sens des mots depuis le XVIe siècle* (Paris: E. Droz, 1934), pp. 172-173.

[51]Curtius, op. cit., p. 69, n. 15.

[52]Quintilian, op. cit, VI, III (104), p. 497.

[53]Ibid.

[54]Ibid., VI, II (8), pp. 421-423.

[55]Ibid., VI, II (13-17), pp. 423-427.

[56]Ibid., (12), p. 423.

[57]"Even though his [the good man's] imagination lacks artifice to lend it charm, its own nature will be ornament enough, for if honour dictate the words, we shall find eloquence there as well." Ibid., XII, I (30), pp. 371-373.

[58]Cf. ibid., VI, III (12), p. 445: ". . . the possession of some peculiar charm of look or manner [". . . proprius quibusdam decor in habitu ac vultu . . ."], the effect of which is such that the same remarks would be less entertaining if uttered by another."

Chapter III

[1]For a general description of this work as a gymnastic treatise, see Michel Binamé, "La théorie de la gymnastique et de 'l'Art de Sauter' d'Archangelo Tuccaro (1536-1604)," in *The History, The Evolution and Diffusion of Sports and Games in Different Cultures. Proceedings of the 4th International HISPA Seminar, Leuven, Belgium, April 1-5, 1975* (Brussels: Université Catholique de Louvain, 1976), pp. 387-402.

[2]Archange Tuccaro, *Trois Dialogues de l'exercice de sauter et voltiger en l'air, avec les figures qui servent à la parfaite demonstration et intelligence dudit art* (Paris: 1599), p. 2r. All translations of this text are mine.

[3]Ibid., p. 8r.

[4]Ibid., p. 4r.

[5]Ibid., p. 9r.

[6]Ibid., p. 10v.

[7]Ibid., p. 15v.

[8]Ibid., p. 17v.

[9]Tuccaro pretends to derive the word "saut" ("leap") etymologically from within the word "assaults" ("attacks").

[10]Ibid., p. 15r.

[11]Ibid., p. 18v.

[12]Ibid., p. 11r.

[13]Ibid., p. 26r.

[14]Ibid.

[15]Ibid.

[16]Ibid., p. 28v.

[17]Ibid.

[18]Ibid., pp. 29v-29r.

[19]Ibid., p. 45r.

[20]Ibid., p. 46r.

[21]Ibid., p. 4v.

[22]Ibid., p. 46v.

[23]Ibid., p. 4v.

[24]Ibid., p.29v (my emphasis).

[25]Arbeau, *Orch.*, p. 5v; *Evans.*, p. 15.

[26]See Riffaterre, "L 'Intertexte Inconnu," in *Littérature* 41 (fév., 1981), p. 4.

[27]Margot D. Lasher, "A Study in the Cognitive Representation of Human Motion," Diss. Columbia University 1978, p. 17.

[28]Arbeau, *Orch.*, p. 41r; *Evans.*, p. 80.

[29]Ibid., p.43v; *Evans.*, p. 83.

[30]*Nouveau Traité de la civilité qui se pratique en France, parmi les honnêtes gens* (Paris: chez Helie Josset, 1682), p. 42. All translations from conduct literature are my own unless otherwise indicated.

[31]Françoise de Ménil, *Histoire de la danse à travers les âges* (Paris: Alcide Picard et Kaan, 1906), p. 160 (my translation).

[32]John Schikowski, *Geschichte des Tanzes* (Berlin/Leipzig: Buchmeister, n.d.), p. 92 (my translation). See also G. Desrat's entry under "geste" in the *Dictionnaire de la Danse* (Paris: Librairies-Imprimeries Réunies, 1895; rpt. Geneva: Editions Slatkine, 1980), p. 164: "Distinction and simplicity of bearing is very closely related to the art of gestures which resides in the teaching of posture and dance" (my translation).

[33]Rodocanachi, op. cit., p. 569.

[34]"Sur la danse," in *Morceaux extraits du Banquet des savans d'Athenée: par Ad. Hubert* (Paris: Librairie classique de L. Hachette, 1828), p. 271 (my translation).

[35]*Nouveau Traité de la civilité*, p. 43.

[36]N. Baudoin, *De l'Education d'un jeune seigneur* (Paris: chez Jacques Estienne, 1728), p. 243 (my translation).

[37]Arbeau, *Orch.*, p. 3v; *Evans.*, p. 12 (my emphasis).

[38]Montaigne, op. cit, III, V, p. 310; *Frame*, p. 672.

[39]De Ménil, op. cit., p. 162 (my translation).

[40]Arbeau, *Orch.*, p. 25r, *Evans.*, p. 52.

[41]Desiderius Erasmus, *De civilitate morum puerilium . . .* (London: W. de Worde, 1532), pp. 21-22.

[42]C. Calviac, *La civile honesteté pour les enfants avec la manière d'apprendre à bien lire, prononcer . . .* (Paris: 1560), p. XV.

[43]Karl Heinz Taubert, *Höfische Tänze. Ihre Geschichte und Choreographie* (Mainz: B. Schott's Söhne, 1968), p. 18 (my translation). The persistence of a religious code may be noted in Erasmas, op cit., p. 22: "non hic honos tribuitur homini, non meritis, sed deo" ("This respect is not due to men or to merit but to God").

[44]Giovanni Della Casa, *Galateo ovvero de' costumi* (Milan: Mursia, 1971), p. 63. The English is from Robert Peterson's 1576 translation (London: Privately printed, 1892), p. 41.

[45]Arbeau, *Orch.,* p. 27v; *Evans.,* p. 54.

[46]Mme. de Lafayette, "La Princesse de Clèves," in *Romans et Nouvelles* (Paris: Garnier, 1961), p. 261 (my translation and emphasis).

[47]For a survey of the written sources of conduct literature see Philippe Ariès, *L'Enfant et la Vie Familiale sous l'Ancien Regime* (Paris: Seuil, 1960), pp. 429-432 or the English version *Centuries of Childhood. A Social History of Family Life,* trans. Robert Baldick (New York: Vintage Books, 1962), pp. 381-384.

[48]Quintilian, op. cit., VI, III (107), p. 499.

[49]Cited in Harry Carter and H. D. L. Verviliet, *Civilité Types* (Oxford: Oxford University Press, 1966), p. 21 (my emphasis).

[50]Penmanship was a motor skill which presupposed a total mastery of posture. As such, it corresponds to the physical discipline of civility which subordinates gesture to a postural control. "Disciplinary control does not consist simply in teaching or imposing a series of particular gestures: it imposes the best relation between a gesture and the overall position of the body, which is its condition of efficiency and speed . . . Good handwriting, for example, presupposes a gymnastics—a whole routine whose rigorous code invests the body in its entirety, from the points of the feet to the tip of the index finger. The pupils must always 'hold their bodies erect, somewhat turned and free on the left side' . . . A disciplined body is the prerequisite of an efficient gesture." Michel Foucault, *Discipline and Punish. The Birth of the Prison*, trans. Alan Sheridan (New York: Pantheon Books, 1977). p. 152.

[51]Stefano Guazzo, *La Civil Conversatione del Signor Stefano Guazzo . . .* (Venice: Presso Altobello Salicato, 1586), p. 80r.

[52]Tuccaro, op. cit., p. 174r.

[53]Ibid., p. 50v. See also the fourteenth-century *Libro di buoni costumi* of Paolo da Certaldo, ed. by Alfredo Schiaffini (rpt. Firenze: F. Le Monmer, 1945), p. 79. "Cortesia non e altro se non misura, e 'misura dura': e non e altro misura se non avere ordine ne' fatti tuoi" ("Courtesy is nothing else but measure, and 'fixed measure': and measure is nothing else than having order in one's acts").

[54]"Della Moderantia," in *Fiore di virtù* (Florence: Compagnia del drago, 1498: rpt. Florence: Stampa di Turati Lombardi E.C., 1949), chapter 41. The English translation is from *The Florentine Fior di Virtu of 1491* (Philadelphia: Library of Congress, 1950), p. 116. A fleeting reference is made to rhetorical "dispositio" but left undeveloped. "And finally the speaker must well prearrange the order of that which he is going to say, because any speech should be divided in six parts."

[55]Norbert Elias, *La Société de Cour* (Paris: Calmann-Lévy, 1974), p. 273 (my translation).

[56]Erasmus' *Colloquia* is the only text in which fixed turns of phrase are handled as precepts of civility. See "Courtesy in Saluting," in *All the Familiar Colloquies of Desiderius Erasmus* (London: 1725), pp. 21-38. I do not wish to reduce civility to silence. It is nevertheless striking that while precepts for the use of the voice proliferate none of them stipulate the use of a given lexicon. The use of words during the reverence would not alter the parallelism of dance and civility since Arbeau recommends that one speak while dancing: "Devisés gracieusement, et d'une parole doulce et honneste . . . non seulement en cest dance gaillarde, mais aussi en toutes aultres sortes de dances" ("Converse affably in a low, modest voice . . . not only when you are dancing the galliard but in performing all other kinds of dance as well"). *Orch.,* p. 63r; *Evans.,* pp. 118-119.

[57]Maurice Magendie, *La Politesse Mondaine et les théories de l'honnêteté en France au XVIIe siècle, de 1600 à 1660* (Geneva: Slatkine Reprints, 1970), p. 150 (my translation). Ariès has also remarked on the content of precepts common to both sub-genres. "It is extremely difficult, with the countless manuals of etiquette produced from the sixteenth century on, to distinguish between those intended for adults and those intended for children." Op. cit., p. 119.

[58]Cicero, *De Officiis* (Cambridge: Harvard University Press, 1975), I, XXXV, pp. 130-131.

[59]See Anthony Lévi, S.J., "The Cult of Glory," in *French Moralists. The theory of the Passions, 1585 to 1649* (Oxford: at the Clarendon Press, 1964), pp. 177-201. See also Octave Nadal, "L'Ethique de la gloire au Dix-Septième siècle," in *Mercure de France* (January-April, 1950), vol. 308, pp. 22-34; and Andre Chastel's remarks on the "conversion au social" and the replacement of public and private virtues by ostentation in the Renaissance in "L'Ostentation, La Passion et la Folie," in *L'Umanesimo e 'La Follia'* (Rome: Abete, 1971), p. 132.

[60]Cicero, op. cit., I, XXVII (94), pp. 96-97.

[61]Della Casa, op. cit., p. 32.

Chapter IV

[1]See Brainard, *Chor.*, pp. 300-301. When I speak of the vertical posture in the following pages I am not referring to the distinction Brainard makes between verticality and horizontality. Verticality, for Brainard, signifies the dancer's individual ornamentation emerging from the uniform horizontality of choreographic pattern. See *Chor.*, pp. 150-151 and p. 222.

[2]Erasmus, *De civilitate,* p. A.7.

[3]Guazzo, op. cit., p. 81v.

[4]Erasmus, op. cit., p. B.7.

[5]Nicolas Faret, *L'Honeste Homme ou, l'art de plaire à la cour* (Paris: chez Jean Brunet, 1639), p. 195.

[6]Erasmus, op. cit., p. A.3.

[7]Ibid., p. A.4.

[8]Ibid.

[9]Ibid., p. C.7.

[10]Ibid., p. B.4. Erasmus considers clothes as an extension of the body. ". . . Vestis quodàmodo corporis corpus est,et ex hac quoque licet habitum animi conicere" (". . . Clothes are in some way the body's body and give an idea of the inner man"). Op. cit., p. B.3. Arbeau writes in the same vein, ". . . quand vous danserez en compagnie ne baissez point la teste pour contrerooler vos pas et veoir si vous dansez bien" (". . . when you dance in company never look down at your feet to see whether you are performing the steps correctly"). *Orch.*, 63v; *Evans.*, p. 118.

[11]Arbeau, op. cit., p. 30v; *Evans.*, p. 59.

[12]Erasmus, op. cit., p. A.3.

[13]Calviac, op. cit., p. xiiij.

[14]Ibid.

[15]Ibid.

[16]Erasmus, op. cit., p. A.4.

[17]Ibid., p. A.6.

[18]Ibid.

[19]Ibid., p. A.7.

[20]I.G.G.D.L.L.: R, *Traicte' de la Phisionomie, c'est à dire, la science de cognoistre le naturel et les complexions des personnes* (Paris: chez Michel Daniel, 1619), p. 5.

[21]Tuccaro, op. cit., p. 41v (my emphasis).

[22]Ibid., p. 33r.

[23]Ibid., p. 41r.

[24]Ibid., pp. 33v-33r.

[25]Ibid., p. 42v.

[26]Arbeau, *Orch.*, pp. 63v-63r; *Evans.*, p. 118.

[27]Ibid., p. 2r; *Evans.*, p. 11.

[28]Ibid., p. 63r; *Evans.*, pp. 118-119.

[29]Ibid., p. 40r; *Evans.*, p. 79.

[30]Ibid., p. 30v; *Evans.*, p. 59.

[31]Ibid., p. 28v; *Evans.*, p. 55.

[32]Fabritio Caroso, *Della Nobiltà di Dame* (Venice: 1600; rpt. Bologna: Forni Editore, 1970), p. 22. The question of the apprenticeship of a second nature will be taken up in the following pages.

[33]Arbeau, *Orch.*, p. 29v; *Evans.*, p. 57.

[34]Ibid., p. 39v; *Evans.*, pp. 76-77.

[35]Ibid.; *Evans.*, p. 77.

[36]Tuccaro, op. cit., pp. 18r-19v. Examples of this condemnation abound. "Est-il possible." writes Jacques Tahureau, "d'appercevoir un plus grand signe de folie que de voir sauter des personnes les unes contre les autres, comme s'ils avoyent l'esprit ravy et troublé..." ("Can you imagine a more patent sign of folly than to see people jumping against one another as if they were totally out of their minds . . ."). *Les Dialogues* (Lyon: 1602), p. 113 (my translation). Similarly, in Erasmus' *De civilitate,* the repetition of sudden, abrupt movements takes on the character of a generalized vice and the definition of vice itself becomes gradually departicularized as madness.

[37]Lambert Daneau, *Traite des Danses, Auquel est amplement resolue la question, a savoir s'il est permis aux Chretiens de danser* (Geneva: 1580), p. 9 (translations from this work are mine).

[38]Ibid., p. 14.

[39]Ibid.

[40]Ibid., p. 16.

[41]Ibid., p. 15. "The denunciation of madness," points out Michel Foucault, "becomes a general form of criticism." See *Histoire de la Folie, p.* 24 (my translation). If dancing was obviously the result of some effort and study, it could be attacked as vanity. "Or si le sauteler et gambader est une chose de soy desja trop folle, voire, et mal convenable: avoir mis ceste vanité en art, et aller à l'eschole pour l'apprendre n'est-ce pas la vanité des vanitéz?" ("Jumping and cavorting about are already mad things and, indeed, most unsuitable: to make of this vanity an art and to go to school to learn it, is this not the vanity of vanities?"). Daneau, op. cit., p. 16.

[42]Montaigne, op. cit., II, X, p. 452; *Frame.,* p. 299.

[43]Ibid., p. 453; *Frame.,* p. 299.

[44]Ibid.; *Frame.,* p. 300.

[45]Ibid., III, XIII, p. 565; *Frame.,* p. 848. See also II, XVII, p. 52. "Au corps mesme, les membres qui ont quelque liberté et jurisdiction plus particulière sur eux, me refusent par fois leur obeyssance, quand je les destine et attache à certain point et heure de service nécessaire" ("Even as regards my body, the parts that have some particular freedom and

jurisdiction over themselves sometimes refuse to obey me when I destine and bind them to a certain time and place for compulsory service"). *Frame.*, p. 493.

[46]Tuccaro, op. cit., p. 41r.

[47]Erasmus, op. cit., p. A.4.

[48]Ibid., p. A.5.

[49]Ibid.

[50]Ibid., p. A.6.

[51]Ibid.

[52]Ibid.

[53]Ibid., pp. A.6-A.7.

[54]Ibid., pp. A.4-A.5 (my emphasis).

[55]Arbeau, *Orch.*, p. 63r; *Evans.*, p. 118.

[56]Quintilian, op. cit., XI, III (68), p. 281. "Decor quoque a gestu atque motu venit."

[57]"Grace is the aesthetic of *ease* . . . It is composed of a technique of inner certainty." Raymond Bayer, *L'Esthétique de la Grâce* (Paris: Alcan, 1933), p. 209 (my translation).

[58]Montaigne, op. cit., II, XVII, p. 33; *Frame.*, pp. 479-480.

[59]Arbeau, *Orch.*, p. 5r; *Evans.*, p. 16.

[60]Montaigne, op. cit., I, XIV, pp. 46-47; *Frame.*, p. 32. See also, III, XIII, p. 538. "La plus contraire qualité à un honneste homme, c'est la delicatesse et obligation à certaine façon particuliere; et elle est particuliere si elle n'est ploiable et souple" ("The most unsuitable quality for a gentleman is overfastidiousness and bondage to certain particular ways; and they are particular if they are not pliable and supple"). *Frame.*, p. 830.

[61]Baldesar Castiglione, *Le Parfait Courtisan du comte Baltazar Castillonois, es deux langues, respondans par deux colomnes, l'une à l'autre, pour ceux qui veulent avoir l'intelligence de l'une d'icelles* (Lyon: Jean Huguetan, 1584), pp. 65-66. *The Book of the Courtier*, trans. Charles S. Singleton (New York: Anchor Books, 1959), I, 26, p. 43. (referred to hereafter in notes as *Singleton*).

[62]Ibid., p. 68; *Singleton.*, I, 27, p. 44.

[63]Faret, op. cit., pp. 26-27. Cf. the moral to Perraults's *Cendrillon:* "La bonne grâce est le vrai don des Fées; Sans elle on ne peut rien, avec elle, on peut tout" ("Graciousness is the true gift of the Fairies. Without it, one can do nothing; with it, one can do all"). *Contes* (Paris: Gallimard, 1981), p. 177; *Perrault's Complete Fairy Tales* (New York: Dodd, Mead and Co., 1961), p. 70. Indeed, in the morality, the magical transformations of the wand are called "dressage" ("training") and "instruction."

[64]Ibid., p. 27. It is evident in Guazzo that imitation is a proliferating interaction: "Queste sono cose, che s'imparano non tanto leggendo, quanto conversando; percioche quando altri parla, noi comprendiamo quel che diletta e quel che spiace, onde sappiamo quel che fuggire, e quel seguirare; si come parlando noi, e veggendo alcuno di quelli, che ci ascoltano poco attento, dalla sua scostumatezza impariamo il modo, che dobbiamo tenere noi nell'ascoltare altrii" ("These are things that are learned less in reading than in conversing; because when others speak we understand what pleases and displeases and so we know what to avoid and what to follow as when we speak and notice that our listeners are inattentive, we learn from their attitude how we should behave in listening to others"). Guazzo, op. cit., p. 81v.

[65]Guazzo, op. cit., p. 70r.

[66]Ibid., p. 71v.

[67]"The aesthetics of the reabsorption of controls." Bayer, op. cit., p. 171 (my translation).

[68]"The domain of spontaneity suddenly broadens to include all controls in the name of *sprezzatura.* Watchfulness, in its turn, becomes spontaneous . . . control, having been transfigured, begins to rival the verve of verve." Ibid., p. 167 (my translation).

[69]"The contrary of orthodoxy is madness." Legendre, op. cit., p. 55 (my translation).

[70]See his *Sir Walter Ralegh, the Renaissance Man and his Roles* (New Haven and London: Yale University Press, 1973), especially pp. 33-40, for a discussion of the relationships of "individual self-fashioning" to the roles which society imposes on Renaissance man.

[71]Arbeau, *Orch.,* p. 40v; *Evans.,* p. 78.

[72]Ibid., p. 48r; *Evans.,* p. 91.

[73]Pierre Charron, *De la Sagesse* (1601; rpt. Geneva: Slatkine Reprints, 1968), I, VI, pp. 32-33 (my translation).

[74]Ibid., II, III, p. 73 (my translation and emphasis).

[75]Castiglione, op. cit., p. 28; *Singleton.,* p. 44.

[76]Arbeau, *Orch.,* p. 27r; *Evans.,* p. 55.

[77]See Brainard, *The Art of Courtly Dancing,* pp. 28-29 and *Chor.,* p. 44.

[78]Arbeau, *Orch.,* p. 27r; *Evans.,* p. 55. Copelande writes that "in some places of France they call the reprises desmarches, and *the branle they call conge,* in English, leave." *The Manner to dance bace dances,* pp. 10-11 (my emphasis).

[79]Brainard, *The Art of Courtly Dancing,* p. 30.

[80]Arbeau, *Orch.,* p. 28r; *Evans.,* p. 56.

[81]Quintilian, op. cit., II, XIII (9-10), p. 293 (my emphasis).

[82]Guglielmo Ebreo, *Trattato dell'arte del ballo* (Bologna: Presso Gaetano Romagnoli, 1873), p. 13.

[83]Kinkeldey, op. cit., p. 9.

[84]Domenico, *De arte,* f. 3.

[85]Brainard bears this out in *Chor.,* pp. 224-225. See also her discussion of Guglielmo Ebreo's use of "pieno" and "vuoto" as "leichte und schwere Taktzeiten," in ibid., p. 148.

[86]C. Mazzi, *Il "libro dell'arte del danzare" di Antonio Cornazano,* p. 13.

[87]Ibid., p. 9.

[88]Kinkeldey, op. cit., p. 10, n. 2.

[89]Inglehearn and Forsyth, op. cit., pp. 37-38.

[90]Guglielmo Ebreo, op. cit., p. 19.

[91]Mazzi, op. cit., p. 9.

[92]Piacenza, op. cit., f. 2.

[93]Ibid.

[94]Brainard, *Chor.,* p. 285.

[95]Arbeau, *Orch.,* pp. 48r-49v; *Evans.,* p. 92 (my emphasis).

[96]Brainard, *Chor.,* pp. 300-301. I would tend to see it rather as the persistence of a common theory not necessarily applied to the same steps.

[97]Rudolf zur Lippe, *Naturbeherrschung am Menschen I* (Frankfort am Main: Syndikat Reprise, 1979), p. 177. "Fantasmata und posata bedingten einander." (my translation).

[98]Piacenza, op. cit., f. 1.

[99]Brainard, *The Art of Courtly Dancing,* p. 53.

[100]Mazzi, op. cit., p. 11. Brainard speaks of the non-movement as satisfying the "aiere" rule whereas it appears that "air" is a function of the return *to* movement, the falcon's flight from stone.

Chapter V

[1]"The difference is that between windy oratory, adroitly playing for effect, and a sound common sense anchored in the substance of experience." Lievsay, op. cit., p. 42. Richard Auernheimer writes, "*La Civil Conversatione* is a book conceived by human concerns, not by the concerns of a beautiful society. Stefano Guazzo was not in search of the ideal man, he was not portraying a 'Cortegiano' ". *Gemeinschaft und Gespräch. Stefano Guazzos Begriff der 'Conversatione Civile'* (Munich: Wilhelm Fink, 1973), p. 52 (my translation). Many misreadings of Guazzo are due in large part to an insufficient awareness of the tradition of *civilitas* essential to both authors.

[2]Michael Riffaterre, *Semiotics of Poetry* (Bloomington and London: Indiana University Press, 1978), p. 81. See also Riffaterre's "Sémiotique Intertextuelle: l'interprétant," in *Rhétoriques, sémiotiques (Revue d'esthétique, 1-2)* (Paris: Collection 10/18, 1979), p. 133. Examples of oratory as a descriptive system for the dance in the French sociolect can be found well into the nineteenth century. Stendhal calls good orators "beaux danseurs," for example in *Lucien Leuwen* (Paris: Le livre de poche, 1960), p. 591.

[3]Louis Marin, *La Critique du Discours* (Paris: Editions de Minuit, 1975), p. 56 (my translation).

[4]Guazzo, op. cit., p. 78v.

[5]"The descriptive system is a network of words associated with one another around a kernel word, in accordance with the sememe of that nucleus. Each component of the system functions as a metonym of the nucleus. So strong are these relationships that any such metonym can serve as metaphor for the ensemble, and at any point in the text where the system is made implicit, the reader can fill in the gaps in an orderly way and reconstitute the whole representation from that metonym . . ." Michael Riffaterre, *Semiotics of Poetry*, pp. 39-40.

[6]Arbeau, *Orch.*, p. 27r; *Evans.*, p. 55.

[7]Ibid., p. 29r; *Evans.*, p. 58.

[8]Ibid., p. 49r; *Evans.*, pp. 92-93.

[9]Guazzo, op. cit., p. 77r.

[10]Ibid.

[11]Ibid., p. 76r.

[12]ibid., p. 78v.

[13]Ibid., p. 79v.

[14]Cicero, op. cit., I, XXXVII, p. 135. In this chapter, Cicero applies the rules of oratory to conversation.

[15]Guazzo, op. cit., p. 79r.

[16]Ibid., pp. 80v-80r. The pertinence of the voice to a theory of dance is underlined by the double use to which Quintilian puts the term measure. During his discussion of variety in eloquence, the preoccupations of the orator are likened to those of the musician: rhythm and tone. Rhythm is said to consist in measure [*modulatione*] and tone in sound and song. Nevertheless, measure is also said to be the principle of vocal inflection: "It is by the raising, lowering or inflexion of the voice that the orator stirs the emotions of his hearers, and the measure, if I may repeat the term, of voice or phrase differs according as we wish to rouse the indignation or the pity of the judge. For, as we know, different emotions are roused even by the various musical instruments, which are incapable of reproducing speech." Op. cit., IX (25-26), p. 171. Thus, in dance treatises, measure as a movement quality rather than a purely metric notion corresponds to the extension of the term measure to vocal inflection in rhetoric.

[17]See Paolo Valesio, *Novantiqua. Rhetorics as a Contemporary Theory* (Bloomington: Indiana University Press, 1980), pp. 127-128. Hirschman points out that the politics of

Renaissance courtliness derive from a reflection on statecraft while not being synonymous with it. *The Passions and The Interests. Political Arguments for Capitalism before its Triumph* (Princeton: Princeton Unversity Press, 1978), p. 13.

[18]Historically speaking, the sovereign was in a position to require others to dance. See Marcel Paquot, "Madame de Rohan Auteur de Comédies-Ballets? (Analyse de trois textes du XVIᵉ siècle), "in *Revue Belge de Philologie et d'Histoire* (1929). vol. VII, no. 8, pp. 805-806.

[19]Montaigne, op. cit., III, VII, p. 354; *Frame.,* p. 702.

[20]Ibid., II, XVII, p. 32; *Frame.,* p. 479.

[21]Ibid., III, IX, p. 408; *Frame.,* p. 740. As Baltasar Gracian put it most cynically, "quiconque honore est honoré. La galanterie et la civilité ont cet avantage que toute la gloire en reste à leurs auteurs" ("whoever honors is honored. Galanterie and civility share the advantage that all glory redounds to their authors"). *L'homme de cour* (1637; rpt. Paris: Editions Champ Libre, 1972), p. 57.

[22]Guazzo, op. cit., p. 72v.

[23]Ibid., p. 72r.

[24]Ibid., p. 73v.

[25]Ibid., pp. 73v-74r.

[26]Ibid., p. 73r.

[27]It is evident in Guazzo's text that "costumi" denotes "qualità" because the two terms appear as doublets. The use Montaigne makes of "moeurs" indicates that it also designates external acts: "Je vois, non une action, ou trois, ou cent, mais des meurs en usage commun et receu" ("I see not one action, or three, or a hundred, but morals in common and accepted practice"). Op. cit., III, IX, p. 394; *Frame.,* p. 730.

[28]Guazzo, op. cit., pp. 73r-74v.

[29]Ibid., pp. 80r-81v.

[30]Ibid., p. 74v.

[31]Ibid.

[32]Ibid., p. 75v.

[33]Ibid., pp. 75r-76v.

[34]"Apres tout, selon que je m'entends en la science du bien-faict et de recognoissance, qui est une subtile science et de grand usage, je ne vois personne plus libre et moins endebté que je suis jusques à cette heure. Ce que je doibts, je le doibts aux obligations communes et naturelles" ("... As far as I understand the science of benefaction and gratitude, which is a subtle science and of great utility, I see no one freer and less indebted than I am up to this point. What I owe, I owe to the ordinary and natural obligations"). Montaigne, op cit., III, IX, p. 407; *Frame.,* p. 739.

[35]Guazzo, op. cit., p. 75r.

[36]Ibid., p. 77r.

[37]Michel Foucault's analysis of sixteenth-century economic theory coincides with my reading of the financial code in Guazzo: "... The metal appeared only as a sign for measuring wealth, in so far as it was itself wealth. It possessed the power to signify because it was itself a real mark." *The Order of Things. An Archaeology of the Human Sciences* (New York: Pantheon Books, 1970), p. 169. On the relationship of coins to the legitimacy of power in the context of royal historiography, see Louis Marin, "The Inscription of the King's Memory: on the Metallic History of Louis XIV," in *Yale French Studies,* 59 (1980), pp. 17-36.

[38]Nicolas Pasquier, *Le Gentilhomme* (Paris: J. Petit-Bas, 1611), CXVI, pp. 41-42 (my emphasis and translation).

[39]Montaigne's distinction between pleasure and profit as affection and glory or power serves to confirm my analysis from within the Renaissance sociolect: "Si elle [la nature] m'eust faict naistre pour tenir quelque rang entre les hommes, j'eusse esté ambitieux de me

faire aymer, non de me faire craindre ou admirer. L'exprimeray je plus insollament? J'eusse autant regardé au plaire que au prouffiter" ("If it [nature] had brought me into the world to hold some rank among men, I should have been ambitious to make myself loved, not to make myself feared or admired. Shall I express this more insolently? I should have thought as much of giving pleasure as of gaining profit"). Op. cit., III, IX, p. 410; *Fame.,* p. 741.

[40]Ibid., p. 393; *Frame., p. 729.*

[41] See in particular the chapter Paul Bouissac devotes to Tuccaro in *La Mesure des Gestes. Prolègomènes à la sémiotique Gestuelle* (The Hague: Mouton, 1973). He asks first, "how can one translate such movements and attitudes into the words and syntax of natural language?", p. 26. He subsequently abandons the linguistic problematic in favor of a hypothetical mathematization of gesture: "It was essential to translate the problem posed into mathematical terms and thereby to arrive at the construction of a model which might permit us to wrest the real from the empire of illusions of a knowledge of techniques unfolding in the descriptions and systems of symbolic notation," p. 174 (my translation). See also, on the subject of gestural semiotics, *Langages* 10 *(Pratiques et Langages Gestuels)* (June 1968).

BIBLIOGRAPHY

Alain. *Système des beaux-arts.* Paris: Gallimard, 1926.

Amyot, Jacques. *Projet de l'Eloquence Royale, composé pour Henry III, roi de France.* Versailles: chez Lamy, 1805.

Angenot, Marc. "Les Traités de l'éloquence du corps," in *Semiotika,* 8 (1973), 60-82.

Apologie de la jeunesse, sur le fait et honneste recreation des danses: contre les calomnies de ceux qui les blasment. Anvers: Chez Gregoire Balthasar, 1572.

Arbeau, Thoinot [Jean Tabourot]. *Orchesographie. Et Traicte en Forme de Dialogue, par lequel toutes personnes peuvent facilement apprendre et practiquer l'honneste exercice des dances.* Lengres: Jehan des preyz, 1589; rpt., Bologna: Forni Editore, 1969.

‒‒‒‒‒‒‒‒. *Orchesography.* Trans. Mary Stewart Evans. New York: Dover Publications, Inc., 1967.

Arena, Antonius de. *Ad Suos Compagnones, qui sont de persona friantes, bassas Dansas et Branlos practicantes novellos, perquamplurimos mandat.* Paris: Chez Philippes Gaultier, 1533.

Ariès, Philippe. *L'Enfant et la vie familiale sous l'Ancien Régime.* Paris: Seuil, 1973.

‒‒‒‒‒‒‒‒. *Centuries of Childhood. A Social History of Family Life.* Trans. Robert Baldick. New York: Vintage Books, 1962.

Aristotle. *"Art" of Rhetoric.* Trans. J. H. Freese. Cambridge: Harvard University Press, 1975.

L'Art du Ballet des origines à nos jours. Paris: Editions du Tambourinaire, 1952.

Atheneus. "Sur la Danse," in *Morceaux extraits du Banquet des savans d'Athenée; par Ad. Hubert,* p. 271. Paris: Librairie Classique de L. Hachette, 1828.

Attaignant, Pierre. *Preludes, chansons and dances.* Paris: 1529-1530; rpt. Neuilly-sur-Seine: Société de Musique d'Autrefois, 1964.

Auernheimer, Richard. *Gemeinshaft und Gespräch, Stefano Guazzos Begriff der "Conversatione Civile".* Munich: Wilhelm Fink, 1973.

Aurigemma, Marcello. "La Civile Conversazione e i Trattati sul Comportamento," in *Letteratura Italiana Laterza,* 19 (1973), 175-213.

Baldwin, Charles S. *Ancient Rhetoric and Poetic.* New York: Macmillan, 1924.

Barthes, Roland. "L'ancienne rhétorique, aide-mémoire," in *Communications,* 16, (1970), 172-229.

Baudoin, N. *De l'Education d'un jeune seigneur.* Paris: Chez Jacques Estienne, 1728.

Bayer, Raymond. *L'Esthétique de la Grâce.* 2 vols. Paris: Alcan, 1933.

Beaujoyeulx, Baltasar, de. *Balet Comique de la Royne.* 1582; rpt., Binghamton: Medieval and Renaissance Texts and Studies, 1982.

Beaumont, Cyril W. *A Bibliography of Dancing.* London: The Dancing Times Ltd.,1929.

Benveniste, Emile. *Problèmes de linguistique générale.* Paris: Gallimard, 1966.

Béranger de la Tour d'Albennas. *Choréide, Autrement, Louenge du bal.* Lyon, 1556.

Bernard, Michel. *L'Expressivité du Corps. Recherche sur les fondements de la théâtralité.* Paris: Delarge, 1976.

Bie, Oskar. *Der Tanz.* Berlin: Julius Bard, 1919.

Bierlaire, Franz. "Erasmus at school: The 'De Civilitate Morum Puerilium Libellus,' " in *Essays on the Works of Erasmus.* Ed. Richard L. De Molen. New Haven and London: Yale University Press, 1978, 239-251.

Binamé, Michel. "La théorie de la gymnastique de 'L'Art de Sauter' d'Archangelo Tuccaro (1536-1604)," in *Proceedings of the 4th International HISPA Seminar, Leuven, Belgium, April 1-5, 1975.* Brussels: Université Catholique de Louvain, 1976, 387-402.

Boiseul, Jean. *Traitte contre les danses*. La Rochelle: 1606.

Boissier, Gaston. *De la signification des mots Saltare et cantare Tragoediam*. Paris: Didier, 1861.

Boissière, Jehan-François de. *Traité de Balet*. Paris: Iliazd, 1953.

Bömer, Aloys. "Anstand und Etikette nach den Theorien der Humanisten," in *Neue Jahrbücher für das Klassische Altertum, Geschichte und Deutsche Literatur und für Pädagogik*, 14 (1904), 223-285, 330-355, 361-390.

Bonicatti, Maurizio. "Le Concept de la déraison dans la tradition de la culture musicale non religieuse à l'époque de l'Humanisme," in *Folie et Déraison à la Renaissance*. Brussels: Université de Bruxelles, 1976, 11-26.

Bouissac, Paul. *La Mesure des gestes: prolégomènes à la sémiotique gestuelle*. The Hague: Mouton, 1973.

Bowra, Sir Maurice. "La danse, l'art dramatique et la parole," in *Le Comportement rituel chez l'homme et l'animal*. Ed. Julian Huxley. Paris: Gallimard, 1971.

Brainard, Ingrid. "Die Choreographie der Hoftänze in Burgund, Frankreich und Italien im 15. Jahrhundert." Dissertation: Göttingen Phil. Fak. of Georg August Universität, 1956.

----------. "Bassedanse, Bassadanza and Ballo in the 15th Century," in *Proceedings of the Second conference on Research in Dance*. New York: CORD, 1970, 64-79.

----------. "The Role of the Dancing Master in Fifteenth Century Courtly Society," in *Fifteenth Century Studies*, 2, (1979), 21-44.

----------. *The Art of Courtly Dancing in the Early Renaissance*. West Newton, Mass: I. G. Brainard, 1981.

Burckhardt, Jacob. *The Civilization of the Renaissance in Italy*. 2 vols. New York: Harper Colophon Books, 1958.

Caillois, Roger. *Les Jeux et les hommes*. Paris: Gallimard, 1958.

Calviac, Claude Hours de. *La civile honesteté pour les enfants avec la manière d'apprendre à bien lire, prononcer . . . Paris, 1560*.

Caroso, Fabritio. *Il Ballarino, diviso in due Trattati Nel primo de' quali si dimostra la diversita de i nomi, che si danno a gli atti, movimenti, che intervengono ni i Balli: e con molte Regole si dichiara con quali creanze, e in che modo debbano farsi*. Venice: Francesco Ziletti, 1581.

----------. *Della Nobiltà di Dame*. Venice: 1600; rpt. Bologna: Forni Editore, 1970.

Carter, Harry and Verviliet, H.D.L. *Civilité Types*. Oxford University Press, 1966.

Casa, Giovanni Della. *Galateo Ovvero de' Costumi*. 1558; rpt. Milan: Mursia, 1971.

----------. *Galateo, of Manner and Behaviours in Familiar Conversation*. Trans. Robert Peterson. 1576; rpt. privately, 1892.

Castiglione, Baldesar. *Le Parfait Courtisan du comte Baltazar Castillonois, es deuz langues, respondans par deux colomnes, l'une à l'autre, pour ceux qui veulent avoir l'intelligence de l'une d'icelles*. Lyon: Jean Huguetan, 1584.

----------. *The Book of the Courtier*. Trans. Charles S. Singleton. New York: Anchor Books, 1959.

Castor, Grahame. *Pléiade Poetics. A Study in Sixteenth-Century Thought and Terminology*. Cambridge, Eng.: Cambridge University Press, 1964.

Celler, Ludovic. *Les Origines de l'Opéra et le Ballet de la Reine (1581): etude sur les danses, la musique, les orchestres et la mise en scène au XVI siècle*. Paris: Didier, 1868.

Certaldo, Paolo da. *Libro di buoni costumi*. Ed. Alfredo Schiaffini. Florence: R. Le Monmer, 1945.

Certeau, Michel de. *L'Ecriture de l'histoire*. Paris: Gallimard, 1975.

----------. "Des Outils pour ecrire le Corps," in *Traverses*, 14-15 (April, 1979), 3-14.

Charbonnel, Raoul. *La Danse*. Paris: Garnier Frères, 1916.

Charron, Pierre. *De la sagesse*. Geneva: Slatkine Reprints, 1968.

Chartier, R., Compère, M.M., and Julia, D. *L'Education en France du XVIe au XVIIIe siècle*. Paris: Sedes, 1976.

Chastel, Andre. "L'Ostentation, la passion, la folie," in *L'Umanesimo e "la follia,"* Rome: Abete, 1971, 129-35.

Chateau, Jean. *Montaigne, psychologue et pédagogue*. Paris: J. Vrin, 1971.

Christout, Marie-Françoise. *Le Ballet de Cour de Louis XIV, 1643-1672. Mise en scènes*. Paris: A. et J. Picard, 1967.

Cicero. *De Inventione*. Trans. S.M. Hubbell. Cambridge: Harvard University Press, 1976.

----------. *De Oratore*. 2 vols. Trans. H. Rackham. Cambridge: Harvard University Press 1976.

----------. *De Officiis*. Trans. Walter Miller. Cambridge: Harvard University Press, 1975.

Ciolek, C.M. "Human Communicational Behavior, A Bibliography," in *Sign Language Studies*, 6 (1975), 1-64.

Closson, Ernest, ed. *Le Manuscrit dit des Basses Danses de la Bibliothèque de Bourgogne*. Brussels: Société des Bibliophiles et Iconophiles de Belgique, 1912; rpt. Geneva: Minkoff, 1976.

Cohen, Selma Jeanne. *Next Week, Swan Lake. Reflections on Dance and Dances*. Middletown: Wesleyan University Press, 1982.

Compagnon, Antoine. *La Seconde Main; ou le travail de la citation*. Paris: Seuil, 1979.

----------. *Nous, Michel de Montaigne*. Paris: Seuil, 1980.

Conté, Pierre. *Danses anciennes de cour et de théâtre en France*. Paris: Dessain et Tolra, 1974.

Copelande, Robert. *The Manner to dance Bace dances*. London: Pear Tree Press, 1937.

Cornazano, Antonio. *Libro dell'arte del danzare*. 1455; rpt. by C. Mazzi in *La Bibliofilia*, 1 (April, 1915), 1-30.

----------. *The Book on the Art of Dancing*. Trans. M. Inglehearn, P. Forsyth. London: Dance Books Ltd., 1981.

Corso, Rinaldo. *Dialogo del Ballo*. Venice: Bordogna, 1555.

Crane, Frederick. *Materials for the Study of the 15th-Century Basse Dance. Studies and Documents 16*. Rome: American Institute of Musicology, 1968.

Curtius, Ernst Robert. *European Literature and the Latin Middle Ages*. Princeton: Princeton University Press, 1973.

Dainville, François de. *La Naissance de l'humanisme moderne*. Paris: Beauchesne, 1940.

Daneau, Lambert. *Traite des Danses, Auquel est amplement resolue la question, a savoir s'il est permis aux Chretiens de danser*. Geneva, 1580.

Davies, Sir John. *Orchestra or, A Poem of Dancing*. Ed. E.M.W. Tillyard. New York: Dance Horizons Republications, n.d.

Delumeau, J. *La Civilisation de la Renaissance*. Paris: Arthaud, 1967.

Desmouliez, M. "Comparaison entre le style et le corps humain," in *Revue des Etudes Latines*, 33 (1955), 59.

Desrat, G. *Dictionnaire de la Danse: historique, théorique, pratique et bibliographique depuis l'origine de la danse jusqu'à nos jours*. Paris: Librairies-Imprimeries Réunies, 1895; rpt. Geneva: Slatkine, 1980.

Dix-Septième Siècle. Rhétorique du geste et de la voix à l'Age Classique. No. 132, 33 année, no. 3 (Juillet-Septembre, 1981).

Dolmetsch. Mabel. *Dances of Spain and Italy from 1400 to 1600*. New York: Da Capo Press, 1975.

----------. *Dances of England and France, 1450-1600*. New York: Da Capo Press, 1976.

Domenico da Piacenza. *De arte saltandi e choreas ducendi*. Paris: Bibliothèque Nationale de Paris, Ms. it. 972.

Doutrepont, Georges. *La littérature française à la cour des Ducs de Bourgogne.* Paris: Honoré Champion, 1909.

Dumur, Guy, ed. *Histoire des spectacles.* Paris: Gallimard, 1965.

DuVair, Guillaume. *De l'éloquence françoise et des raisons pourquoy elle est demeurée si basse.* Paris: A. L'Angelier, 1606.

Elias, Norbert. *La Civilisation des moeurs.* Paris: Pluriel, 1973.

—————. *The History of Manners.* New York: Pantheon Books, 1982.

Erasmus, Desiderius. *Declamatio de Pueris statim ac liberaliter instituendis. Etude critique, traduction et commentaire par Jean-Claude Margolin.* Geneva: Droz, 1966.

—————. *De civilitate morum puerilium per Des. Erasmum Roterodamum, Libellus nunc primum et conditus et aeditus . . .* London: W. de Worde, 1532.

—————. *La Civilité Puérile.* Ed. Philippe Ariès. Paris: Ramsay, 1977.

—————. *The Familiar Colloquies of Desiderius Erasmus of Roterdam.* Trans. N. Bailey. London: 1725.

Faret, Nicolas. *L'Honeste Homme ou, l'art de plaire à la cour.* Paris: Chez Jean Brunet, 1639.

Felice, Philippe de. *L'Enchantement des danses et la magie du verbe. Essai sur quelques formes inférieures de la mystique.* Paris: Albin Michel, 1957.

Fiore di Virtù. Florence: Compagnia del drago, 1498; rpt. Florence: Stampa di Turati Lombardi E.C., 1949.

Fletcher, Ifan Kyrle. *Bibliographical Descriptions of forty rare books relating to the art of dancing in the collection of P.J.S. Richardson, O.B.E..* London: The Dancing Times, Ltd., 1954.

The Florentine Fior di Virtu of 1491. Trans. Nicholas Fersin. Washington: Library of Congress, 1953.

Foclin (Fouquelin), Antoine. *La Rhétorique française d'Antoine Foclin.* Paris: André Wechel, 1555.

Foucault, Michel. *Histoire de la folie à l'âge classique.* Paris: Gallimard, 1972.

—————. *Les Mots et les choses.* Paris: Gallimard, 1966.

—————. *The Order of Things. An Archaeology of the Human Sciences.* New York: Pantheon Books, 1970.

—————. *Surveiller et punir. naissance de la prison.* Paris: Gallimard, 1975.

—————. *Discipline and Punish. The Birth of the Prison.* New York: Pantheon Books, 1977.

Gardiner, H.M. *Feeling and Emotion, A History of Theories.* Westport, Connecticut: Greenwood Press, 1970.

Genette, Gérard. *Introduction à l'architexte.* Paris: Seuil, 1979.

Gray, Hannah H. "Renaissance Humanism: the Pursuit of Eloquence," in Paul Oscar Kristeller and Philip P.Wiener, ed. *Renaissance Essays from the Journal of the History of Ideas.* New York: Harper and Row, 1968.

Gracian, Baltasar. *L'Homme de Cour.* 1637; rpt. Paris: Champ Libre, 1972.

Guazzo, Stefano. *La Civil Conversatione del Signor Stefano Guazzo Gentilhuomo di Casale di Monserrato, divisa in quattro libri.* Venice: Presso Altobello Salicato, 1586.

—————. *La Civile Conversation, dividée en quatre livres.* Trans. Gabriel Chappuys. Lyon: Jean Beraud, 1579.

Guglielmo Ebreo. *Trattato dell'arte del Ballo.* Bologna: Presso Gaetano Romagnoli, 1873.

Guilcher, Jean-Michel. *La Contredanse et les renouvellements de la danse française.* The Hague: Mouton, 1969.

—————. "Les différentes lectures de l'Orchesographie de Thoinot Arbeau," in *La Recherche en Danse,* 1 (1982), 39-49.

----------. "L'Interprétation de l'orchésographie par des danseurs et des musiciens d'aujourd'hui," in *La Recherche en Danse,* 2 (1983), 21-32.

Guillemin, A.-M. "Cicéron et Quintilien," in *Revue des Etudes Latines,* 37 (1959), 184-194.

Gunther, Helmut. "Ballet de cour: Beginn einer selbstbewussten Ballettkunst," in *Das Tanzarchiv,* 5 (1973) 137-142.

Hayes, Frances. "Gestures: A Working Bibliography," in *Southern Folklore Quarterly,* 21 (December, 1957), 218-317.

Heartz, Daniel. "The Basse dance. Its Evolution circa 1450 to 1550," in *Annales Musicologiques,* 6 (1958-1963), 287-340.

Hennebert, F. *Histoire des traductions françaises d'auteurs grecs et latins pendant les XVIe et XVIIe siècles.* Brussels, 1861; rpt. Amsterdam, 1968.

Heuss, Alfred. "Eine Vorführung altfranzösischer Tänze in Dresden," in *Zeitschrift der Internationalen Musikgesellschaft,* 11, 12 (1910), 386-389.

Hirschman, Albert O. *The Passions and the Interests. Political Arguments for Capitalism before its Triumph.* Princeton: Princeton University Press, 1978.

Huguet, Edmond. *L'Evolution du sens des mots depuis le XVIe siècle.* Geneva: Droz, 1967.

Huizinga, Johan. *Homo Ludens: A Study of the Play Element in Culture.* Boston: the Beacon Press, 1955.

I.G.G.D.L.L.:R. *Traicte' de la Phisionomie, c'est à dire, la science de cognoistre le naturel et les complexions des personnes . . ..* Paris: Chez Michel Daniel, 1619.

Jackman, James L. *Fifteenth Century Basse Danses.* Wellesley College, 1964.

Jouanna, Arlette. *Ordre Social. Mythes et Hierarchies dans la France du XVIe siècle.* Paris: Hachette, 1977.

Jousse, Marcel *l'Anthropologie di Geste.* 3 vols. Paris: Gallimard, 1974.

Kinkeldey, Otto. "A Jewish Dancing Master of the Renaissance: Guglielmo Ebreo," in *A.S. Freidus Memorial Volume.* New York: 1929; rpt. New York, Dance Horizons, 1972.

Kristeva, Julia. *Sèméiotikè. Recherches pour une Sémanalyse.* Paris: Seuil, 1969.

Lafayette, Mme de. "La Princesse de Clèves," in *Romans et Nouvelles.* Paris: Garnier, 1961.

Lancelot, Francine. "Ecriture de la danse. Le système feuillet," in *Ethnologie Française,* 1 (1971), 29-58.

Langages 10. *(Pratiques et Langages Gestuels).* (June, 1968).

Lanham, Richard A. *The Motives of Eloquence. Literary Rhetoric in the Renaissance.* New Haven: Yale University Press, 1976.

La Noue. *Discours Politiques et Militaires.* 1590; rpt. Geneva: Droz, 1967.

Lasher, Margot D. "A Study in the Cognitive Representation of Human Motion." Ph.D. Dissertation: Columbia University in New York, 1978.

Lausberg, Heinrich. *Handbuch der Literarischen Rhetorik.* Munich: Max Huever, 1973.

Lauze, François de. *Apologie de la Danse. Et la Parfaicte Methode de l'Enseigner tant aux Cavaliers qu'aux Dames.* 1623; rpt. London: Frederick Muller, Ltd., 1952.

Lee, Rensselaer, W. *Ut Pictura Poesis: the Humanistic Theory of Painting.* New York: W.W. Norton and Co., 1967.

Le Faucheur, Michel. *Traitté de l'action de l'orateur ou de la pronociation et du geste.* Paris: Augustin Combe, 1657.

Lefevre, Abbe Pierre. *Le Grant et vray art de pleine retorique: utille proffitable et necessaire a toutes gens qui desirent a bien elegantement parler et escripre.* Paris: J. Longis, 1534.

Legendre, Pierre. *L'Amour du Censeur: Essais sur l'Ordre Dogmatique.* Paris: Seuil, 1974.

----------. *La Passion d'être un Autre, Etude pour la danse.* Paris: Seuil, 1978.

Le Guern, Michel. *Sèmantique de la mètaphore et de la mètonymie.* Paris: Larousse, 1973.

Lettres Patentes du Roy, pour l'établissement de l'Academie Royale de la Danse en la ville de Paris. Paris: Pierre le Petit, 1663.

Levi, Anthony. *French Moralists: the Theory of the Passions, 1585-1649.* Oxford: Clarendon Press, 1964.

Lievsay, John Leon. *Stefano Guazzo and the English Renaissance, 1575-1675.* Chapel Hill: the University of North Carolina Press, 1961.

Lucian. "The Dance (Saltatio)," in *Lucian.* Cambridge: Harvard University Press, 1955. Vol. V.

Luz, Maria. "Le Ballet et ses Débuts en Europe," in *Jardin des Arts,* 19 (1956), 426-432.

Magendie, Maurice. *La Politesse mondaine et les théories de l'honnêteté, en France au XVIIe siècle, de 1600 à 1660.* Geneva: Slatkine Reprints, 1970.

Marrocco, W. Thomas. *Inventory of 15th Century Bassedanze, Balli and Balletti.* New York: CORD, 1981.

Marin, Louis. *Etudes sémiologiques.* Paris: Klincksieck, 1971.

----------. "Les Corps utopiques Rabelaisiens," in *Littérature,* 21 (1976), 35-51.

----------. *La Critique du Discours.* Paris: Editions de Minuit, 1975.

----------. "The Incription of the King's Memory: on the Metallic History of Louis XIV," in *Yale French Studies,* 59 (1980), 17-36.

Mary, André. "'L'Orchésographie de Thoinot Arbeau," in *Les Trésors des Bibliothèques de France.* Ed. E. Dacier. Paris: 1935.

Mauss, Marcel. "Les Techniques du corps," in *Sociologie et Anthropologie.* Paris: P.U.F., 1950.

McGowan, Margaret M. *L'Art du Ballet de Cour en France, 1581-1643.* Paris: C.N.R.S., 1978.

Ménestrier, Le. P. Claude-François. *Des Ballets Anciens et Modernes selon les Regles du Theatre.* Paris: chez Rene' Guignard, 1682.

Michel, Arthur. *Die Altesten Tanzlehrbücher.* Brunn: Rudolf M. Rohrer, n.d.

Miller, James L. "Choreia: Visions of the Cosmic Dance in Western Literature from Plato to Jean de Meun." Dissertation: Toronto, 1979.

Montaigne, Michel de. *Essais.* Paris: Garnier Frères, 1962.

----------. *The Complete Essays of Montaigne.* Trans. Donald M. Frame. Stanford: Stanford University Press, 1957.

Nadal, Octave. "L'Ethique de la gloire au dix-septième siècle," in *Mercure de France,* 308 (January-April 1950), 22-34.

Negri, Cesare. *Le Gratie d'Amore di Cesare Negri Milanese, detto il Trombone, Professore di ballare, Opera Nova, et Vaghissima, divisa in Tre Trattati.* Milan: 1602; rpt. Bologna: Forni Editore, 1969.

Nouveau traité de la Civilité qui se pratique en France, parmi les honnêtes gens. Paris: chez Helie Josset, 1682.

Noverre, Jean Georges. *Lettres sur la Danse et les Arts Imitateurs.* 1760; rpt. Paris: Ed. Lieutier, 1953.

Panzer, Marianne. *Tanz und Recht.* Frankfurt am Main: Moritz Diesterweg, 1938.

Paquot, Marcel. "Madame de Rohan, auteur de Comédies-Ballets?," in *Revue Belge de Philologie et d'Histoire,* 8 (1929), 801-829.

----------. "La Manière de composer les ballets de cour d'après les premiers théoriciens français," in *Cahiers de l'Association Internationale des Etudes Françaises,* 9 (June, 1957), 183-197.

Paradin, Guillaume. *Le Blason des Danses.* Beau-ieu, 1556; rpt. Paris: Firmin Didot, 1830.

Paris: Bibliothèque Nationale de Paris, Manuscript Division, MS. Ital. 476. Giovanni Ambrosio.

Pascal, Blaise. *Pensées et opuscules*. Paris: Hachette, 1971.

Pasquier, Nicolas. *Le Gentilhomme*. Paris, 1611.

Perrault, Charles. *Contes*. Paris: Gallimard, 1981.

————. *Perrault's Complete Fairy Tales*. New York: Dodd, Mead and Co., 1961.

Petermann, Kurt. *Tanzbibliographie*. 10 vols. Leipzig: Bibliographisches Institut, 1965-1970.

Physiologus. Trans. Michael J. Curley. Austin and London: University of Texas Press, 1979.

Pickard-Cambridge, A.W. *Dithyramb Tragedy and Comedy*. Oxford: at the Clarendon Press, 1927.

Porta, Jean Baptiste. *La Physionomie Humaine*. Trans. Rault. Rouen: Jean et David Berthelin, 1655.

Pouilloux, Jean-Yves. *Lire les "Essais" de Montaigne*. Paris: Maspero, 1969.

Prunières, Henry. *Le Ballet de Cour en France avant Benserade et Lully, suivi du Ballet de la Délivrance de Renaud*. Paris: Henri Laurens, 1944.

Quintilian. *The Institutio Oratoria of Quintilian*. Trans. H.E. Butler. London: William Heinemann, Ltd.; Cambridge, Massachusetts: Harvard University Press, 1969.

Rabelais, François. *Oeuvres complètes*. Ed. Jacques Boulenger and Lucien Scheler. Paris: Editons Gallimard, 1955.

Refuge, Eustache de. *Traicte de la Cour, ou Instruction des Courtisans*. Paris: C. Barbin, 1664.

Reyna, F. *Des Origines du Ballet*. Paris: A. Tallone, 1955.

Richter, Mario. *Giovanni Della Casa in Francia nel secolo XVI*. Rome: Edizioni di Storia e Letteratura, 1966.

Ricoeur, Paul. *La Métaphore vive*. Paris: Seuil, 1975.

————. *The Rule of Metaphor*. Toronto and Buffalo: University of Toronto Press, 1977.

Riffaterre, Michael. *Essais de stylistique structurale*. Paris: Flammarion, 1971.

————. *Semiotics of Poetry*. Bloomington and London: Indiana University Press, 1978.

————. *La Production du texte*. Paris: Seuil, 1979.

————. "Sémiotique intertextuelle: l'interprétant," in *Rhétoriques, sémiotiques (Revue d'esthétique)*. Collection 10/18. Paris, 1979, pp. 128-150.

————. "Syllepsis," in *Critical Inquiry*, 6 (Summer 1980), 625-638.

————. "La trace de l'intertexte," in *La Pensée*, 215 (October, 1980), 4-18.

————. "L'Intertexte inconnu," in *Littérature*, 41 (February, 1981), 4-7.

Rigolot, François. *Poétique et onomastique. l'exemple de la Renaissance*. Geneva: Droz, 1977.

Rodocanachi, E. "La Danse en Italie du XVe au XVIIIe siècle," in *La Revue des Etudes Historiques*, 7 (Nov.-Dec. 1905), 569-590.

Ryngaert, J.-P. "Un Exemple de codification du jeu de l'acteur au XVIe siècle: le théâtre de Gérard de Vivre," in *Revue d'Histoire Littéraire de la France*, 2 (March-April, 1972), 193-201.

Sachs, Curt. *World History of the Dance*. New York: W.W. Norton, 1937.

Saint Hubert. *La Manière de Composer et Faire Reussir les Ballets*. Paris: chez François Targa, 1641.

Santosuosso, Antonio. *The Bibliography of Giovanni Della Casa. Books Readers and Critics, 1537-1975*. Florence: Leo S. Olschki, 1979.

Schikowski, John. *Geschichte des Tanzes*. Berlin and Leipzig: Buchmeister, n.d.

Stendhal. *Lucien Leuwen*. Paris: Livre de Poche, 1960.

Struever, Nancy S. *History in the Renaissance. Rhetoric and Historical Consciousness in Florentine Humanism*. Princeton: Princeton University Press, 1970.

Tahureau, Jacques. *Les Dialogues*. Lyon, 1602.

Taubert, Karl Heinz. *Höfische Tanze. Ihre Geschichte und Choreographie.* Mainz: B. Schott's Söhne, 1968.

Thibault, Jacques. *Les Aventures du corps dans la pédagogogie française.* Paris: J. Vrin, 1977.

Toulouze, Michel. *L'Art et Instruction de Bien Dancer.* Paris: 1488; rpt. London: Emery Walker Ltd., 1936.

Traité de la Civilité nouvellement dressé d'une manière exacte et méthodique et suivant les regles de l'usage vivant. Lyon: J. Certe, 1689.

Traité de la Comédie et des Spectateurs, Selon la Tradition de l'Eglise, Tirée des Conciles et des Saints Peres. Paris 1669.

Trattati d'Amore del Cinquecento. Ed. Guiseppe Zonta. Bari: Scrittori d'Italia, 1912.

Trexler, Richard. *Public Life in Renaissance Florence.* New York: Academic Press, 1980.

Tuccaro, Archange. *Trois Dialogues de l'Exercice de Sauter et Voltiger en l'Air, avec les Figures qui servent à la Parfaite Démonstration et Intelligence Dudit Art.* Paris, 1599.

Tyard, Pontus de. *Les Discours Philosophiques de Pontus de Tyard.* Paris: A. l'Angelier, 1587.

Ulmann, Jacques. *De la gymnastique aux sports modernes. Histoire des doctrines de l'education physique.* Paris: J. Vrin, 1977.

Valesio, Paolo. *Novantiqua. Rhetorics as a Contemporary Theory.* Bloomington: Indiana University Press, 1980.

Vasari, Georgio. *Le Vite dei Più eccelenti pittori, scritori e architetti.* Florence: G. Sansoni, 1906.

Verwey, H. de la Fontaine. "The first 'book of etiquette' for children: Erasmus' 'De Civilitate morum puerilium,'" in *Quaerendo,* 1 (1971), 19-30.

Vigarello, Georges. *Le Corps Redressé. Histoire d'un Pouvoir Pédagogique.* Paris: Delarge, 1978.

Viguerie, Jean de. *L'Institution des Enfants. L'Education en France. 16e-18e siècle.* Paris: Calmann-Levy, 1978.

Woodhouse, J.R. *Baldesar Castiglione: A Reassessment of the Courtier.* Edinburgh: Edinburgh University Press, 1978.

Wundt, Wilhelm. *The Language of Gestures.* Paris: Mouton, 1973.

Yates, Frances A. *The Art of Memory.* London: Routledge and Kegan Paul Ltd., 1966.

Zuccolo da Cologna, Simeon. *la Pazzia del Ballo.* Padua, 1549.

Zur Lippe, Rudolf. *Naturbeherrschung am Menschen.* 2 Vols. Frankfurt-am-Main: Syndikat Reprise, 1979.